WHAT READERS ARE SAYING

"Bonnie Harvey's book, *Living Life Twice: A Second Chance at Adulthood,* is filled with real life stories and realistic, practical suggestions on how to start over and get a second chance. Any adult who has faced disappointments, losses, or unexpected tragedies will be inspired to adapt to life's changing circumstances with a positive attitude based on Bonnie's encouraging advice and Bible-based wisdom. A gem of a book and a guide to enjoying life to the fullest with maturity and wisdom."

Judy Nichols, Author
Teaching in Tough Times, Titanic A to Z,
and *Titanic* ˄ ˄ *the Rescue*

"Dr. Bonnie ⟨...⟩ iring and practical book i⟨...⟩ reader a keen sense of ho⟨...⟩ rdless of the adversity tha⟨...⟩ ner. Bon-  nie uses the real ⟨...⟩ ˅ ˅ ˅(s) of others in bringing an additional sense of genuineness to the book. The chapter regarding Andrew Carnegie in rediscovering yourself through the importance of giving over receiving really hit home with me. *Living Life Twice* is rich in insight and it empowers the reader on his/her journey toward emotional and spiritual wholeness."

Hiram Keith Johnson, LCSW, Author
Tragic Redemption: Healing the Guilt and Shame

"Change is hard on everybody, but devastating changes can bring you to your knees and fill you with hopelessness. In *Living Life Twice: A Second Chance at Adulthood,* Bonnie talks about the unexpected death of her husband in her middle years and her determination to embrace a second chance at adulthood. Her book is filled with practical advice from her experiences and the inspirational lives of famous achievers from America's history. Bonnie artfully weaves scripture through every chapter quoting the promises of God and letting her readers know that no matter what the circumstances with God all things are possible.'"

Sarah Norkus, Author
The Secret Diary of Sarah Chamberlain (2012)
The Secret Treasure of Battersea (2014)

Using a potent mix of personal testimony from the remembrances of a young Bonnie Harvey earning money picking berries to historical perspectives, the author illustrates the advantages of mature wisdom—especially following a tragedy. Too often, people give up and quit living when they encounter grief and loss. The author shows how various well-known people like Colonel Sanders (Kentucky Fried Chicken) and Helen Keller have overcome their disadvantages. Told with insight and humor, persistent optimism, and practical advice, *Living Life Twice: A Second Chance at Adulthood,* points the way to a productive second adult life.

Terry Bailey, Author
The Pilate Plot and *The Malachi Mysteries*

Living Life
TWICE

Living Life
TWICE

A Second Chance at Adulthood

Bonnie C. Harvey

*To Steven –
God bless you
always!
In Friendship –
Bonnie C. Harvey
– 12-14-13 –*

LANGMARC
PUBLISHING

Austin, Texas

LIVING LIFE TWICE
A Second Chance at Adulthood

By Bonnie C. Harvey

Cover layout: Michael Qualben
Cover art: © Sally Gutzke

Scripture quotations with permission from the
NIV Textbook Bible (Zondervan), Grand Rapids, MI, 1984.
The Living Bible (Tyndale House Publications), Wheaton IL, 1973
The New Testament in Modern English, J. B. Phillips (MacMillan, NY) 1960.
The Message Bible, by Eugene H. Peterson (Navpress Publishing Group), Colorado Springs, CO, 2002.
The King James Bible, 1611

Published by LangMarc Publishing
P.O. 90488
Austin, TX 78709
www.langmarc.com

Library of Congress Control Number: 2013948369
ISBN: 1-880292- 53-X

DEDICATION

To my brothers—

Dr. Douglas Gary Carman, Ph.D., Distinguished Professor Emeritus of Finance and Economics, Texas State University, Retired.

Dr. Neil Jon Carman, Ph.D., Botany. Clean air program director for the Lone Star Chapter of the Sierra Club.

Thank you for the love and support
you have shown me through trying times.

CONTENTS

FOREWORD

I have known Bonnie Harvey for many years. She is a woman who chooses joy. As life has given me many challenges, Bonnie has been an example of a woman who never gave into self-pity but sought to be all God intended her to be. She never quit! She gave me courage.

In the '60s, she and her husband, Ray, recent converts to Christ, came to Montreat to talk with my grandfather as they sought to determine God's will for their lives. They decided to live in Montreat so he could pursue a college degree. I first knew Bonnie as the mother of my best friend in grade school. Having left a lucrative business she and Ray took a job as dorm parents at a local college to help make ends meet. As girls, her daughter, Cindy, and I would buzz around the small community on our bicycles. We talked for hours about the things young girls talk and giggle about. We played around the college dorm and she taught me how to roller-skate. Later we even tried ice-skating on frozen Lake Susan! Fun years...

As a young woman I was often in their home. She and her husband, Ray, were eager students of the Bible and helped disciple me around their dining table. They had a strong conviction that the Bible was the inspired, authoritative Word of God. It was central to their home. I treasure the copy of J. B. Phillips' *The New Testament in Modern English* they inscribed and gave to me. Bonnie always treated me as a friend - not just her daughter's friend, but her friend as well. She honored me with her respect.

From a close vantage point I observed her as a young mother and wife, a businesswoman and student, they always had some business venture going to try to augment their income as students. I saw her struggles to adjust from a suburban homemaker to dorm mother of dozens. She had to adapt to an income that didn't meet the needs. Always I saw her live with integrity and a smile.

After a few years they moved away so Ray could begin seminary training; I didn't see them as often. Cindy and I grew apart but Bonnie and I stayed in touch – mainly through her writing and publishing endeavors as I was, by then, an acquisitions editor for Harper & Row. From time to time we'd meet up in a city and catch up over lunch – like the friends we were. She always encouraged me to develop my mind – to reach farther. She believed in me.

Bonnie is a remarkable person. Her life was not easy. She had to "reinvent" herself many times as her role shifted around her family. She was eager to be the best wife and mother she could be. But her life didn't turn out the way she expected it to.

When Ray died suddenly, it was a huge loss for the family. He was a man with a larger than life personality. He was the kind of person who got things done. But his death also gave Bonnie the opportunity to develop who she was as a person – no longer in the shadows. I think many of us can identify with that – I know I can.

She grabbed life by the horns and met the challenges – which were many – head on. She never indulged in self-pity or had a "woe is me" attitude. As I said earlier, she chose joy. And through it all she learned – she went back to school all the way to get her Ph.D. degree! She was a published movie critic earning the respect and trust of many. But mostly she was a student of God. She learned His truths and she applied them to her life.

In this book she shares what she learned through it all. I don't enjoy books that unload all sorts of heady knowledge without a shred of applicability. This delightful book is very readable, inspiring and practical. Bonnie lets you look over her shoulder as she discovers great practical, applicable truths. You will come to love and appreciate her as I do.

Buy this book. Read and learn from my cherished friend – she has walked this unpredictable path called life. And has done so choosing joy!

Ruth Graham
Author, *In Every Pew Sits a Broken Heart*
and Founder of Ruth Graham Ministries

PREFACE

Life "happens" and many people experience tragedies, reversals of fortune, losses, and disappointments in their lives during their middle years and beyond. As traumatic as the event may be, what happens afterwards can be even more tragic for those who believe "You only live once." Surrendering to bitterness or regret can end your life before it's over. With God's help and your own determination, you not only can make it through your circumstances but come out a better, more balanced person than before.

People live longer lives today than they did 50 years ago. Instead of wasting their years of maturity and wisdom, they need to use and enjoy them. *Living Life Twice: A Second Chance at Adulthood* will encourage people to realize their lives aren't over following their loss. By facing and acknowledging the Difficulties, then taking steps to develop the Action Plan, a person recovering from loss can achieve the Benefits of living life twice.

Why is this book needed?

Today's headlines are full of stories about people challenged by the sluggish economy. In addition, we hear of the "fallout" from the economic slowdown, such as mental and physical health problems, broken homes, even suicides. Too often people just "stop living" when tragedy strikes. They are so overcome with grief, self-pity, and frustration, they don't know what to do. *Living Life Twice* can guide these individuals to a spiritual victory over their hardships and teach them positive responses to life's difficulties. By looking to their strengths and overcoming their weaknesses, people devastated by life events can discover the best years of their lives. The writer shares her personal experiences to convey a message of hope to those who read this book.

ACKNOWLEDGMENTS

Margaret Lease, Voice Teacher Extraordinaire. In loving memory of your joyous spirit, and for encouragement and motivation—even when I hadn't practiced.

Dr. Jim and Cindy Fletcher, my children. Thank you for continued support and putting up with my idiosyncrasies.

Cecil Murphey. Author, *90 Minutes in Heaven*. Thanks for your home critique group early writing help and continuing encouragement.

Gloria, Brenda and Nola, part of the critique group that met in my home. Thanks for input on my writing projects—even when it hurt.

Susan Bass, Program Chair at Kennesaw University Continuing Education. Thanks for working with me in your cheerful, optimistic way and always providing me with a lectern with the KSU logo for my classroom.

The students in my classroom, at KSU, Life Enrichment and DeKalb Medical Wellness Center. Thanks for the patience you have shown your teacher. I wish you Godspeed and blessings in your own writing.

Dr. Victor Kramer, Ph.D., English, and Thomas Merton Scholar. Thanks for being exactly the right person at the right time for my doctoral dissertation.

DeKalb Medical Wellness Center—Director of Community Outreach, Gail Winston; and Office Coordinator, Conchata Wells. Thanks for implementing my writing courses into your already great curriculum.

Dr. Sharon King, Ph.D. Gerontology and Editorial Assistant. Thanks for your invaluable editorial help.

Connie Kepros, number #1 fan from my Iowa home town. Thanks for having faith in me and helping find book shelf space in my hometown library for my books.

Terry Bailey, Hiram Johnson, Judy Nichols, and Sally Norcus. Thanks for the gracious things you've said in your Endorsements for my book. Thanks, too, to Ruth Graham for encouragement in her Foreword to my book. May the kind words you've spoken prove to be true. Thanks as well to Artist Sally Gutzke for her innovative cover design.

Lois Qualben—Thanks for editorial suggestions, help, and encouragement, plus having faith in my book project.

To my deceased sister, Dorothy, and brothers, Ken, Don, and Ron. Also, to my deceased son, Steven. Your lives were cut so short! But I thank God for the life He gave each of you. You will always remain in my memory. You are missed.

INTRODUCTION

A Second Chance

I. Acknowledge the Difficulties

A. *I'm faced with too many decisions* – Making Good Choices

B. *I don't deserve what's happened to me* – Avoiding Self-Pity

C. *I'm running out of money* - Managing Finances

D. *No one understands what I'm going through* – Avoiding Isolation/Loneliness

E. *I can't go on—this trial is too difficult* – The Challenges of Adversity

F. *I don't need anyone's help* – Seeking Support

G. *What will I do when others find out what has happened* – The Difficulties with Pride and Reputation

H. *I'm too old to deal with this* – Facing Your Aging Process

I. *My health is failing* – Coping with Health Problems

J. *Nothing seems to work* - Dwelling on Negatives

II. Positive Responses – Developing an Action Plan

A. *I can get through this* - Finding Your Strength and Willpower

B. *It's too soon to give up* - Determining to Succeed

C. *First things first* - Setting up Guidelines

D. *I know God's listening* - Asking God's Help and Guidance

E. *This won't defeat me* - Not Letting Life's Disappointments Take Over

F. *There's no shame in asking for help* – Accepting Help from Others

G. *If at first I don't succeed, Try, Again* - Re-thinking Solutions

H. *No more junk food* - Eating Wisely

I. *I have to get off this couch* - Getting Regular Exercise (Walking)

J. *This could be so much worse* - Maintaining a Positive Outlook

K. *Someone may need my help* - Reaching Out to Others

III. The Benefits of "Living Twice"

A. *There's more to me than I thought* - Rediscovering Yourself

B. *I haven't tried that before* - Learning New Things/Learning New Skills

C. *There's much I can learn in all this* - Growing Mentally, Emotionally, and Spiritually

D. *I do have a choice* - Doing What You Want

E. *I can do this!* - Attaining a Sense of Accomplishment/Gaining Self Confidence

F. *This is only making things worse* - Changing Habits—for the better

G. *I'm not too old to learn* - Taking a Class

H. *Time to get over this* - Accepting What Cannot Be Changed

IV. Conclusion – The Second Time Around

CHAPTER ONE

LEARNING TO CHOOSE WISELY

"If Life had a second edition, how I would correct the proofs."

John Clare (1793-1864)

My Story

Little did I realize when my life changed suddenly in my middle years that I was being offered a second chance at adulthood. A second chance to correct some of the mistakes I'd made earlier in my first life, but also the opportunity to move forward and become my own person.

This time I possessed the maturity and knowledge to make good, objective decisions. In addition, I had moved from being an Idealist and Romantic to being pretty much a hard-core Realist. Things are the way they are, and I would have to make decisions based on the facts. No Prince Charming would come and sweep me off my feet. But actually, I'm not sure I'd desire that anyway. If Prince Charming did come, at best it would be a stopgap. Later on, I'd still have to deal with ME and my own set of circumstances.

When my husband died suddenly some years ago, overnight I became my sole breadwinner and a U.S. taxpayer. Oh, I had worked at a few jobs here and there, but nothing to constitute gainful employment. Besides,

1

when my husband lived, I could always ask for extra money and get it. Now, that source had been removed. In addition, my husband had tapped into his life insurance policy only a few weeks before his untimely death and the money quickly evaporated with unplanned expenditures and funeral expenses.

Once the shock of his death wore off, however, I was forced to take stock and decide what I should do next. The conclusion I came to at that time was this: By making a turning point in my life a new beginning instead of a tragic ending, I could experience the challenge and satisfaction of a second adulthood.

How This Book Can Help You

This book shows three steps to "Live Your Life Twice." First, we all have to acknowledge The Difficulties we face. Avoiding them doesn't make them go away. I will discuss ten difficulties many of us face when a disaster strikes. Some of the difficulties in this section include: 1) Making good choices 2) Avoiding self pity 3) Managing finances 4) Avoiding loneliness 5) The Challenges of Adversity 6) Seeking support 7) Disdaining pride 8) Facing your aging process 9) Coping with health problems, and 10) Dwelling on negatives.

One of the most important steps to a new chance for a second adulthood is taking action. In Section II, we look at eleven Positive Responses to difficulties and the action steps we need to take to overcome the difficulties we face. Here are some of the issues I deal with in Section II: 1) Finding your will power 2) Determining to succeed 3) Setting up guidelines 4) Asking God's help and guidance 5) Not letting life's disappointments take over 6) Accepting help from others 7) Re-thinking solutions 8) Eating wisely 9) Exercising regularly 10) Maintaining a positive outlook, and 11) Reaching out to others.

Finally, I show you ten benefits you can discover when you decide to live your life twice. Once you acknowledge your difficulties and take positive action steps, you may be amazed at the beneficial outcomes. Here are a few of the great benefits that can come in the second part of your life: 1) Rediscovering yourself 2) Learning new skills 3) Learning new things 4) Growing mentally, emotionally, spiritually 5) Doing the things you want to do 6) Attaining a sense of accomplishment 7) Growing in self confidence 8) Changing poor habits for better ones 9) Taking a class, and 10) Accepting what cannot be changed.

My own journey toward a second adulthood has been exciting. I realize now I not only can make my own decisions, not having to answer to others, but also that I have the maturity and experience to make good, sound decisions in every area of my life. So, don't let whatever tragedy has happened stop you. Survey your options, think and pray about them; then, get up, dust yourself off, and with new resolve, tell yourself: others have succeeded after experiencing difficulties, and I can too!

Youthful Experiences

As I pondered the path of my new adult life, I remembered some of the foolish things I did in my childhood and teen years. Here are two examples:

"Come on, Mary; it's so hot out, let's go swimming in the Turkey River," I called to my freckle-faced friend.

"Okay, but we'll have to walk, 'cause I don't know of anyone driving that way," she replied, shaking her ash-blond pigtails.

After running to our homes, which were practically next door to each other and putting on swimsuits under our street clothes, the two of us set out on the three-mile trek along the dusty, graveled northeast Iowa road that led to the river. Once we reached the river, we quickly took off our outer clothes and plunged into the cool, refreshing water. Of course, after a rain, the water could also be dark brown and muddy. But we didn't care as we happily dog-paddled in the murky water. Neither one of us could swim, but we managed to stay afloat anyway.

Although we didn't know it, the river also held hidden dangers in addition to the water's depth—which was probably 20 to 30 feet—and also very wide at this spot—at least 400 to 500 feet across. Only a few yards from where we splashed happily, a good-sized whirlpool swirled its eddies just before the water plunged over the dam. We were unaware of the whirlpool but had we paddled a little further in that direction, we would have been caught in it and most likely catapulted to our deaths over the dam. I shudder today when I think of the chance both Mary and I took swimming in the Turkey River on that hot, summer day so long ago.

Another time, the two of us started off on our balloon-tired red and blue bikes to ride to the neighboring town of Decorah, some twenty miles away. Now, nothing much existed between our town and this one. The lush, green landscape was dotted here and there with white frame houses and peaceful farmland with red and white Guernsey cows grazing contentedly in the fields. After we had ridden our bikes about ten miles, Mary and I were tired, hungry, thirsty, and soaked with perspiration. But we still had about ten miles to go!

After a brief rest, Mary cheered both of us when she said, " I have an aunt and uncle living in Decorah. Maybe they will give us a ride back home."

We finally reached our destination late in the afternoon of that warm summer's day in June between riding our bikes and walking. And, fortunately, Mary's relatives took pity on two pre-teenaged girls and gave us a ride back to our homes.

I did learn from this experience, though, to count the cost before you set out to do something. You need to evaluate the project first, then, be sure you can finish what you start. My friend and I also took a chance biking and walking on a lonely, out-of-the way highway where something dreadful could have happened to us. But we were young and inexperienced and had little realization of any potential dangers lurking just beyond the highway.

Of course, I made numerous other poor choices in my growing-up years and beyond, but I have learned from each of them, too. I concur with the statesman, William Pitt as he wished in a House of Commons speech in 1741, "that I may be one of those whose follies may cease with their youth, and not of that number who are ignorant in spite of experience." I hope to be one of those who learn from my experiences—good and bad.

How sobering it is to realize that all of life's big decisions begin with the lesser ones we make along the way. Sometimes, we can rectify the inadequate choices we've made; at other times, we cannot. We are forced to live with the results. At least now, with a clean slate before me as I embark on the second part of my life, I can step back, take my time, examine my options, and decide in a deliberate manner what to do.

This time I have the tools and equipment to make wise, satisfactory choices. What a relief it is not to just drift passively along but to make the proper choice after weighing all the ramifications of my decision—then to be pleased with the outcome.

You can also check out the library and the internet for your topic to see what experts suggest would be right for you. In addition, you can peruse the magazine section at the grocery store (or bookstore) for appropriate articles that often are tailor-made for the subject for which you're seeking a solution.

Another alternative is to ask the advice (carefully!) of family and friends; but be cautious not to let them CHOOSE for you! The final choice should be yours. So you are without excuse now for making an ill-advised decision. After all, this second opportunity at life is too precious to throw away. You need to make the most of it—and that includes making wise decisions.

CHAPTER TWO

AVOIDING SELF PITY

"I don't deserve what's happened to me"

"Our joys as winged dreams do fly;
Why then should sorrow last?
Since grief but aggravates thy loss,
Grieve not for what is past."

Anonymous

Our first reaction to tragedy is usually "Why did this happen to me?" Often, we have no idea as to why something happens; we have to deal with what we can do now that it has happened. Our first emotion is shock, then the mind takes over and we re-examine the events leading to the situation. A sense of loss involves not only death but loss of a job, a relationship, and many other life problems. And, with loss, comes a grieving process.

In my case, I hadn't long to grieve. I had to proceed with getting business affairs in order, then figure out how I would earn a living. I'm thankful in retrospect that that was the case because the situation took my mind off my loss and helped point me to the next step to take. As time passed, though, I had such a sense of "aloneness"; no one was there to advise me as to what to do. I did struggle at times with self-pity but usually talked myself out of it. I also had an overwhelming sense that God had allowed this tragedy to occur in my life, and He would show me what to do. I believe He even whispered to my spirit: "It's sink or swim time now, Bonnie. What are you going to do?"

Not only did I feel "alone" at times but gradually I also sensed a "newness" in my life. As the apostle Peter says in the first chapter of his letter, "For you have a new life. It was not passed on to you from your parents, for the life they gave you will fade away. This new one will last forever, for it comes from Christ, God's ever-living Message to men (I Peter 1:23,TLB).

Two people who exemplify to me a positive outlook on life the second-time around are: Grandma Moses (Anna Mary Robertson Moses) and Colonel Sanders, of Kentucky Fried Chicken fame.

Grandma Moses (1860-1961)

"I, Anna Mary Robertson, was born back in the green meadows and wild woods on a farm in Washington County, in the year of 1860, September 7th, of Scotch Irish ancestry. My ancestors came to this country at different times between 1740 and 1830, all of them settling in the immediate vicinity of southern Washington County, New York State."[1]

Anna Mary, the third of ten children, lived a typical girl's rural life at that time: she helped with the farm chores, attended a one-room country schoolhouse for several months of the year, and at the age of twelve, left home to work as a hired girl on a neighbor's farm. Of average height, Anna Mary had fine, delicate facial features, but also possessed a "no nonsense" look about her. Her hands and fingers were constantly in motion doing the many necessary chores she had to do.

While working as a hired girl in her late twenties, she met and married the love of her life, Thomas Salmon Moses, who also worked as a hired hand. The two moved to different farms, even to one in Virginia, working as tenant farmers until they could afford to buy their own farm. Then in 1905, when Anna Mary was 45 years old, the couple and their children moved back to upstate New York, settling outside the town of Eagle Bridge, not far from Anna Mary's birthplace.

Anna Mary, now affectionately called "Mother Moses," was a determined woman who understood her role as a farm wife and mother. She cooked, cleaned, washed, canned, embroidered, and even wall-papered while raising her own five children (five others had died in infancy). In fact, Mother Moses was incredibly handy all the way around—she was a woman of her time doing all the chores other women did then. She not only worked hard, but she displayed common sense and much ingenuity in performing her various jobs.

A few years earlier, Anna Mary recalls painting her first "large" picture. "One time I was papering the parlor, and I ran short of paper for the fire board. So I took a piece of paper and pasted it over the board, and I painted it a solid color first, then I painted two large trees on each side of it, like butternut trees. And back in it I did a little scene of a lake and painted it a yellow color, really bright, as though you were looking off into the sun light. In the front, to fill in the spaces, I brought in big bushes. I daubed it all on with the brush I painted the floor with."[1a] Painting that scene served to awaken an artistic sense in Anna Mary, and before long the artist in her began to re-surface.

In this setting, probably in the late 1920's and 1930's (in her seventies), Grandma Moses (as she lovingly became known to her extended family), began to concentrate on her artistic interests. Earlier, these interests could be observed in her embroidered pictures and decorative sewing.

In 1938, Louis Calder, an art collector from New
York City, happened upon one of her paintings in a
local drug store window—Grandma was then in her
late seventies. Calder was able to arrange an exhibit for
her work at the Museum of Modern Art in New York
City, although not much came of it. However, a year
later, Otto Kallir, an Austrian immigrant and owner of
Galerie St. Étienne became interested in her work and
arranged a one-woman exhibition in New York City in
October, 1940.

The exhibition, entitled "What a Farm Wife Painted," even caught the attention of Gimbel's Department
Store, and they displayed several of her paintings in
their annual Thanksgiving Festival. Additional exhibi-
tions and press acclaim followed and her success sky-
rocketed. Grandma noted concerning her unusual artistic acclaim: " I am not superstitious or anything like
that, but there is something like an overruling power. I
never thought that I would do such work, I never know
how I'm going to paint until I start in; something tells
me where go right on and do. It was just as though he
[her deceased husband, Thomas] had something to do
about this painting business. I have always thought
ever since, I wonder if he has come back. I wonder if he
is watching over me. "[1b]

By her 100th birthday, September 7, 1960, Governor
Nelson Rockefeller decreed the day as "Grandma Moses Day." She had become one of the most well-known
and beloved artists of her time. She said, however, that
"If I didn't start painting, I would have raised chickens. I can still do it now. I would never sit back in a
rocking chair waiting for someone to help me. I have
often said, before I would call for help from outsiders, I
would rent a room in the city someplace and give pancake suppers, just pancake and syrup, and they could
have water, like a little breakfast."[1c]

Because of the income her paintings generated, however, Grandma Moses never held any "little breakfasts" in the city. When she died the following year at age 101, she left behind her paintings of one small corner of the world: upstate New York in all its seasons. She also left behind an amazing legacy of what one person can accomplish in her later years—all her success came after the age of seventy.

Colonel Harland Sanders (1890-1980)

Harland Sanders, too, achieved fame later in life—after the age of 65—when many people retire. Harland David Sanders was born in a small farmhouse near Henryville, Kentucky, on September 9, 1890. His father died when Harland was just five years old, and he recalls feeling "empty and frightened," and that everything was changing in his life. Soon, his mother found work in Henryville, and Harland was left to take care of his younger brother and sister, which was not that unusual for the time in which they lived.

From then on, even as a young boy when his mother remarried, he decided to strike out on his own. Harland worked at many different jobs from farmhand to being a fireman on a train, to selling insurance, and studying to become an attorney. He did achieve a certain amount of success in each of these fields, but he didn't feel satisfied. In the meantime, he married Josephine King by whom he had three children. Harland always worked hard to do well in whatever job he had, but sometimes his bad temper got the best of him and he lost the job.

During the "Roaring Twenties," Harland formed a ferryboat company, which seemed like a lucrative business to him. The ferryboat, a steel-hulled stern wheel steam boat, could carry 15 cars and 150 people for 10 cents a person and fifty cents a car. Within thirty days, he had sold enough stock to finance the venture, and his commission amounted to $22,000.

Because of his success in this venture, Harland thought his future lay in the business community. So he left for Columbus, Indiana where he applied for the position of Executive Secretary of the Chamber of Commerce. But after getting the job, he realized it offered no real future for him. At the age of thirty-three, Harland Sanders surveyed the prosperous country around him and made up his mind to get in on the prosperity himself. He continued to get into various businesses, even the bootlegging business. Although he did not drink, he helped many drunks get involved with Alcoholic Anonymous.

Then, in the 1930's, Harland opened a restaurant called Sander's Café in central Kentucky. People who ate there commented, "Good place to eat. I'll tell you. Best place around." The café served many different kinds of people from salesmen and locals to students traveling back and forth to area schools.

Sanders Café proved successful almost from its beginning in the Sanders Gas Station, but it was not until a hardware store owner introduced Harland to a "pressure cooker" that Sanders' imagination went into overdrive. He experimented with cooking vegetables and other foods in the cooker—and, of course—chicken, which later became part of the cooking process for his famous Kentucky Fried Chicken.

In 1949, Lt. Governor Lawrence Wetherby bestowed a second Kentucky Colonel commission on Harland. He framed this one, and in time, began to take on the identity of a Kentucky Colonel, dressing in a white suit, and black string tie. Soon, he added a white moustache and goatee to his already white hair.

A short time later, however, he was dealt a terrible disappointment. The Interstate highway planners announced the routing of I-75, the new route Harland himself had pushed for, would by-pass his restaurant.

Then, only the local trade, and not salesmen, travelers, and college students, would frequent his café.

He tried to sell his restaurant without success, so he was forced to auction it off for $75,000. This was at a considerable loss for him. He still had to earn a living, and at 65, he wasn't sure what to do. He was down, but he was not out.

When he received his first social security check for $105, he knew he had to find another way to earn a living. As John Y. Brown, who later bought Kentucky Fried Chicken, said of him, "The wonderful thing about the Colonel is that he never thought of quitting. [Instead, he told himself], 'There's something in this world I can do better than anyone else, and the only thing I can think of is frying chicken, so that's what I'll do.'"[2]

So, he loaded some pressure cookers, timers, and packages of his secret herbs and spices into the trunk of his car and began to sell KFC Franchises all around the Midwest. He slept in the back seat of his car to save motel bills, and as he demonstrated cooking the chicken at different places, ate a constant diet of chicken. He was sixty-five years old, his arthritis hurt him more and more, but there was no way he could be content living on social security. He told himself, "I will make one more start. H—I had to."[2a]

The rest is history. The Colonel lived to be 90 years old; when he died, many honors and accolades were bestowed on him. He is also Kentucky's most famous citizen. Today there are Kentucky Fried Chicken stores worldwide, and he is known and loved in many countries. All his success came after the age of 65; if the Interstate highway had not by-passed his restaurant in Kentucky, none of this would have happened, for his rise to the heights did not even begin until he reached retirement age.

Former Kentucky Governor John Y. Brown summed up Harland Sanders' life when he said, "His life should be a constant reminder to senior citizens that 'the best is yet to be.'"[2b] When members of the United States Congress asked him what one should do to prepare for retirement, he responded, 'Give him an opportunity to do for himself. NEVER STOP WORKING. A man will rust out before he wears out.'"[2c]

Colonel Sanders most likely would tell us the same thing today, and so would Grandma Moses. Who knows what you can yet achieve if you but determine to do so. Maybe in the near future, history will record your story. Or, even better, maybe you have a contribution to make that will help many people. It's up to you.

[1]*Grandma Moses: My Life's History.* Grandma Moses, Harper & Row Publishers, New York, 1952; pp.3, [1a]122, [1b]125, [1c]138.

[2]*The Colonel.* John Ed Pearce. Doubleday & Company, Inc., New York, 1982; pp. 102, [2a]103, [2b]Foreword, [2c]Foreword.

CHAPTER THREE

MANAGING FINANCES

"Help—I'm Running Out of Money!"

"God gave me my money. I believe the power to make money is a gift from God....I believe it is my duty to make money and still more money and to use the money I make for the good of my fellow man according to the dictates of my conscience."

John Davison Rockefeller
(1839-1937)

One of the biggest challenges we face following a calamity is managing the money we have. Similarities between the way we handle money and Rockefeller's in the above quotation rarely exist. From the time he was a young boy, Rockefeller's father encouraged him to keep track of every cent he earned as well as each penny he spent. Although Rockefeller had less than two years of a bookkeeping course, his early habit of paying close attention to money earned and spent started him on his lifelong course of managing money.

John continued these thrifty practices into his young adulthood and beyond. At Central High School in Cleveland, Ohio, young John struggled with some of his lessons, especially spelling, but showed himself to be a stellar student in mathematics. After high school, he paid $40 for a brief bookkeeping course at a college level; then, he needed to find a job.

Into Business

He started his business career, however, at the tender age of seven when he discovered some wild turkey eggs in a nest near his home in upstate New York. His mother, Eliza Davison Rockefeller, urged him to watch the nest until the eggs hatched and the birds were big enough to fatten for market. John followed his mother's advice and kept the proceeds in a blue china jar kept for that purpose. The young Rockefeller was much like his mother not only in her pale and delicate features but in her conscientiousness and serious outlook on life. Through his early poultry sale and other experiences where he made money work for him, John decided this was what he would do— receive interest from monetary investments.

From his early job at Hewitt and Tuttle in 1855 where he worked as a bookkeeper-clerk, similar to the position Bob Cratchit held with Scrooge, John worked his way up the ladder. His tools were a dip pen, ledger, and a blotter. All the items he dealt with had to be carefully printed in precise, legible handwriting and figures, and he reveled in his work.

In time, after doing well in his own commission business, oil was discovered in Pennsylvania. John was in a primary position to take advantage of the discovery with his knowledge of transportation on Lake Erie and the railroads as well as his careful bookkeeping practices. He had also honed his high school debating skills in business as he negotiated with clients. The main use for oil at the time was for kerosene lamps, but everyone used kerosene lamps so business was booming.

But it was Rockefeller's association later with railroad tycoons William H. Vanderbilt and Jay Gould that propelled him into a monopoly with the oil business.

The businessmen's association bought out the smaller oil refineries and cornered "secret preferred rates" to ship the oil out of the oil fields to other markets. As he bought out one refinery after another, John became known as the "anaconda of Standard Oil" and "an Octopus."[3]

By 1880, he refined ninety-five percent of the oil produced in the United States. He was on his way to becoming the richest man in America as well as the most hated. His protégé, Frederick Gates, advised him at that time to start giving his money away because "Your fortune is rolling up, rolling up like an avalanche! You must distribute it faster than it grows! If you do not, it will crush you, and your children, and your children's children."[3a]

John took his wise counsel and ended up endowing numerous colleges, medical facilities, and many other worthwhile causes. His son, John, Jr., was also a philanthropist who commissioned the restoration of Williamsburg, Virginia, the Marble Collegiate Church in NYC, and also Rockefeller Center in NYC. Perhaps Rockefeller's immense success with finances was predicated on a verse from the book of Proverbs—a verse he was fond of quoting: "Seest thou a man diligent in business? He shall stand before kings."[3b]

Berry Pickin'

One of my earliest jobs when I was nine or ten years old was picking strawberries at a nearby Garden Center—Bents Nursery. I would start off early each morning when the dew was still on the grass, wearing a short-sleeved red and white checkered shirt, faded blue jeans, navy keds, and a big, dilapidated straw hat. My two older brothers, Don and Ken, also worked at the nursery. I worked at different jobs like weeding onions and radishes as well as picking berries, but I liked picking strawberries the best in the hot summer months.

I liked this job the best because I could sit down on the ground and pluck the berries. Sometimes I knelt as well to pick the berries. Whichever method I used, the results gave me red, berry-stained knees and red, berry-stained "seat of my pants." The few other girls who picked berries got their clothes dyed, too, from the berry stains. Try as I might, I could not avoid crushing some berries and getting the juice on my clothing.

To my mind, I got paid well for picking the berries: around .03 per box—a pint box, I think. Filling up each box took some time, though, and after a few hours, I might have picked just ten boxes. I also ate some of the plump, juicy berries along the way. The berry boss punched my card for each box, and we got paid in cash every week. The short season for berries lasted only around six weeks or so in June. Sometimes on those hot summer days, Rita or one of the other girls called out to me, "Bonnie, do you want to leave now?" The other girls generally left in the middle of the afternoon, but I had to stay until closing time because of my big brothers' insistence on it.

The raspberry season followed the strawberry season but I didn't like it as well. The prickery branches scratched my arms and even my legs, and I had to remain standing to pick the berries. I spent whatever money I earned picking berries on frivolous items I'm sure, like knick-knacks and candy at the local Woolworth's store. Today I have nothing to show for my berry pickin' days, not even a pair of knee red or "seat" red blue jeans. But it was a good experience for me to break into the capitalist system. One of the important things I learned from my "berry picking" days was the relationship between doing work and getting paid for it. I learned, too, the necessity of stick-to-itiveness because of my older brothers' insistence on my staying in the berry patch 'til closing time. I'm sure I wasn't the best employee for the Nursery owner but I'm grateful today that he put up with me so I could learn some valuable lessons of life.

Baby Sitting

I also did some baby sitting as a young teenager. One job I had was caring for two youngsters: six-year-old, sandy-haired Jimmy, and his eight-year-old, blond sister, Meg. I didn't mind caring for them except for bedtime. Then I would hear, "Bonnie, can I have a drink of water?" Or, "I have to go to the bathroom," usually a half hour after they had just "gone to the bathroom." I wanted to get them to bed and asleep so I could join my friend Margie on the front porch. She lived across the street and came over with a bunch of movie magazines. When the children finally fell asleep, Margie and I would sit on the front porch, pour over the magazines and laugh our hearts out. Fortunately, the parents never came home while my friend and I were giggling on the front porch over the magazines.

When the parents returned, the father, a local dentist, drove me home and paid me less than fifty cents an hour—the going wage at the time, but at least I had some money coming in. Some of the lessons I learned from this job were the responsibility of punctuality and the responsibility of watching over two rambunctious youngsters—especially if we went to the park during a daytime job. Each of the various jobs I had contributed to my overall experience of learning to be a good employee, a desirable lesson to learn.

Managing Your Finances

Your last name may not be Rockefeller, but you can still learn to manage your finances. The first thing you ought to do is to set up some kind of budget or at least write down your income and expenses on a sheet of paper. Put down your expenses on the left side of a 6" x 9" sheet of paper, listing the priority items like

Rent (or mortgage), Utilities, Transportation, Food, Insurance, Taxes, etc. On each side of the items, list the amount owed and the due date for these items. On the right side of the paper, you can list other items that are important but perhaps not crucial to your budget like cable TV or any unexpected bills. Sometimes I use colored pens to write the amount due so it stands out. At the bottom of the page, I insert my expected income, since I am self-employed with a home office. As the bills arrive each month, put them in alphabetical order as to when they're due. I often rubber band or clip the bills together with the budget sheet on top. In addition, I often use a post-it note with the items that might be due for the coming week. That way I can see at a glance what needs to be taken care of soon. Of course, if you bank on line, you may set up a different system. But I will say that I never miss payments and I'm never late. Occasionally there are extenuating circumstances, in which case I always contact my creditor and work out a delayed payment with them. I have found if you're honest with people, they will work with you.

Plant Store Job

Now if your outgo exceeds your income, you'll need to find some employment to compensate. Some years ago when I was in this position, I walked at a nearby mall and stopped at a small, inviting plant store to ask if they needed any help. They did, and I worked part-time off and on for a number of years. The job turned out to be a fairly pleasant one; it was five minutes from my home, and the owners were glad to have me. I was their best "sweeper" having learned from my mother who made me do chores several times until I got them right! I also learned to put manila paper "sleeves" on large corn plants and peace lilies; in addition, I was a frequent cashier where I needed to balance the register down to the last penny. The plant store provided a good outlet for me to get out and be with people as well as bringing in additional income.

Looking at my budget every month, I can quickly determine what I can and cannot afford. That knowledge contributes to my sense of security and peace of mind, and I am grateful. If I start to worry about how I'm going to pay my bills, I turn to the Sermon on the Mount (in Matthew 6:25-33) that says: "Therefore I say unto you, take no thought for your life, what ye shall eat, or what ye shall drink; nor yet for your body, what ye shall put on. Is not the life more than meat, and the body than raiment? Behold the fowls of the air: for they sow not, neither do they reap, nor gather into barns; yet your heavenly Father feedeth them. Are ye not much better than they?..for your heavenly Father knoweth that ye have need of all these things. But seek ye first the kingdom of God, and his righteousness; and all these things shall be added unto you."

As I ponder these verses, I turn the whole situation over to my heavenly Father. I know He cares for me and He will help me. He has yet to fail me. How wonderful to know He will not fail you, either, if you ask Him to help you.

You can also pray this prayer in the little book," *I've Got to Talk to Somebody, God,*" by Marjorie Holmes: "Oh, God, give me more faith in your abundance. Help me to stop worrying about money so much. Let me spend less time fretting about material things....Lord, help me to remember how generously you have endowed the earth. That you have lavished upon us more food than we can consume. More clothing than any of us can wear. More treasures than we can carry. And that it is your will that each of us have his portion. A fine full portion to meet all our needs....For so long as I trust in you all these needs are being, and will be met."[4]

[3]*John D. Rockefeller.* Ellen Greenman Coffey. Silver Burdett Press, Englewood Cliffs, New Jersey, 1989; pp. 67, [3a]90, [3b]28.

[4]*"I've Got to Talk to Somebody, God."* Marjorie Holmes. Doubleday & Company, Inc. Garden City, New York, 1969; pp. 5,6.

Two reference books about money:

What to Do When the Economy Sucks Peter Sanders. FW Media, Inc. Avon, MA, 2009.

Easy Money. Liz Pulliam Weston. Pearson Education, Inc. Upper Saddle River, NJ, 2008.

Chapter Four

Avoiding Isolation/Loneliness

"No one understands what I'm going through"

"If a [person] does not make new acquaintances as he advances through life, he will soon find himself left alone. A [person], sir, should keep his friendship in constant repair."

Samuel Johnson-(1709-1784)

Samuel Johnson, a major British writer and dictionary compiler, knew what he was talking about here—he lived to be 75 years old and no doubt had numerous friends. In 1755, Johnson finished compiling the first English dictionary, which was a remarkable achievement. Because he had trouble finding a publisher, however, he couldn't pay his bills and experienced much poverty in the process. Nevertheless, we owe him a great debt for his compilation of the first English dictionary.

Helen Keller: Epitome of Isolation and Loneliness (1880-1968)

Helen Keller's remark, "Life is either a daring adventure, or nothing at all"[5] proved to be true in her own life. Helen Keller entered the world on June 27, 1880, in Tuscumbia, Alabama as a "seeing, hearing" child.

Like all little children, she had begun to speak words and phrases as a nineteen-month-old little girl. But she contracted what was called a "brain fever" at that age, and by the time the fever left her, she had lost both her eyesight and her hearing. From then on, she became uncontrollable. She lived in a dark world where neither sight nor sound could penetrate. The movie, *The Miracle Worker* portrays the young seven-year-old taking food from the table, knocking into things and creating chaos wherever she went.

Her parents didn't know what to do with her and considered putting her into a mental asylum. Then Helen's parents hired a twenty-year-old teacher, Annie Sullivan, to come to Alabama to work with Helen. Annie began teaching Helen and trying to reach her through "finger talk," a means of communicating with blind/deaf children through finger language. Annie tried to tell Helen that "Everything has a name," but she met with little success at first. One day, however, as Helen remembered the incident later, "Annie took one of my hands and placed it in the cool flow of water [from the pump]. She spelled out 'W-A-T-E-R' in the palm of the other hand." Helen's face lit up as "Suddenly I felt as if somehow the mystery of language was revealed to me. 'WAWA' was that cool something that flowed over my other hand." From then on, Helen could not learn fast enough as she comprehended her world for the first time.

In 1888, Helen traveled to Boston, Massachusetts, with Annie, where she attended the Perkins Institution for the Blind. She was already quite an accomplished reader at this point, reading books in Braille. At age 13, Helen had grown into a lovely teenager—although she never saw her own face.

One of her many accomplishments was learning to read lips. She practiced on Annie, placing her middle finger on Annie's nose, and her forefinger on the lips while resting her thumb on Annie's larynx. Helen wanted to master the "spoken language," too. So in the fall of 1894, she enrolled in the Wright-Humason School for the Deaf in New York City. Her speaking voice, however, sounded "robotical," and she left the school without attaining the quality of speaking voice that she desired.

After graduating from Perkins Institute and the Wright-Humason School for the Deaf, Helen planned to attend college. At the time, though, few young women continued their education beyond high school. Helen, however, was determined. She applied, and was admitted to Radcliffe College, a women's college in Cambridge, Massachusetts.

She was sometimes lonely at Radcliffe. Just one other student knew the finger alphabet, so she found it difficult to make friends. To help her, some kind classmates bought her a Boston Terrier that she named "Phiz." The little dog brought her much pleasure—she could communicate with him without using finger language.

After graduating from Radcliffe in 1904 with honors, she and Annie began to give lectures (her speaking voice did improve some over time). She became known all over the world, meeting with famous people like Mark Twain, the American author. He regarded her as the most remarkable woman he had ever met because of her accomplishments. She also knew Alexander Graham Bell, the inventor of the telephone, and corresponded with him regularly. She signed her letters to him, "Your loving little friend."[5a]

When Annie died in 1936 following a long illness, Helen was at her bedside holding her hand. She said she felt a "loneliness...that will always be immense."[5b]

Helen Keller spent her adult life giving lectures and promoting the causes she believed in. At age sixty-eight, a student asked her, "How do you approach old age?" Helen replied, "There's no age to the spirit."[5c] She died at age eighty-eight, but her unconquerable spirit lives on.

Finding Friends

Although I had older siblings, I was the "baby" of my family for eight years. My sister was in her teens by then, interested in boys and wanted nothing to do with a "bratty" younger sister who "borrowed" everything of hers from curlers to clothes (if they fit!). My older brothers had each other; they, too, didn't want much to do with me. Although at times, they let me play a game of monopoly on their bed. The price I often paid for that privilege was a merciless tickling session. So I was left to fend for myself.

My course of action was simple: make friends with the neighbors. At the age of seven or so, I would march up and down the street, knock on doors, and chat with the people who came to the door. I called on a variety of people. One woman, Mrs. Nicholson, made delicious rosettes. I loved it when she had just made a fresh batch. She made them using some kind of an iron that gave them a unique shape, then dusted them with powdered sugar. She invited me into her kitchen, saying in a thick Norwegian accent, "Come in, Bonnie, and have some just-baked rosettes." Who was I to refuse such an offer?

Other people I visited were: Martha Schmidt and Gretchen Newberg. I used to brush and comb Martha's long hair. She liked having me come to her home to do this task! As for Gretchen, a school teacher, she played all those old timey songs like "I Left My Heart in San Francisco" and "Springtime in the Rockies" on the slightly out-of-tune piano. And, we would sing the songs together. I visited many of the country schools where she taught and envied the students who rode ponies to school and ate mysterious lunches from their lunch boxes (probably peanut butter and jelly sand-wiches). When I visited these schools with my teacher friend, I was treated like a princess—someone who went to city schools. All the children from the first grade through the eighth sat in a good-sized class-room. One time I even attended a basket social at one of Gretchen's schools. It was great fun. Some older gentle-man bought my basket, and of course, I had to sit and eat with him. That was something I never would have experienced if I hadn't knocked on Gretchen's door a few years earlier.

Through my willingness even as a young child to meet new people, I learned some great lessons. Most of the people I met that way often expressed delight at meeting a young girl who gave them company. May-be they were lonely, too. Today, knocking on strange doors involves some risk, but at that time in my life it seemed perfectly natural. I did learn to meet new people through this experience, which was an impor-tant lesson. Most of the people were pleasant and open to me coming to see them. Today, I'm much more cau-tious than I was then.

Making Friends

Many of us, including myself, live in a different lo-cation from the one in which we grew up. The people where we live now don't know our family members and background. This situation means we have to work harder at making new friends.

A few years ago, I had the wonderful experience of having many different people come to my apart-ment for an evening of fun and to hear an inspirational speaker. People came from various places around the city. They often brought covered dishes such as potato salad and fried chicken along with desserts like car-rot cake and chocolate chip cookies. We placed all the food on my little, glass-topped rattan dining table, and the guests naturally chatted around the food and the table. One night, around thirty people gathered in my apartment and we were hard pressed to find a place for everyone to sit. I met many delightful people in my own apartment from these events. I have also made new friends by joining church choirs, writing groups, speaker groups (like Toastmasters), and other groups. If you seek out a group where you live, you can usually find a place where you'll fit in. By doing so, you'll avoid the feelings of loneliness and isolation that can plague people as they move from place to place. The main thing to remember is an axiom from the Bible: "A man who has friends must himself be friendly" (Proverbs 18:24, NKJV).

Combating Loneliness

Other ways to deal with loneliness are: (1) Acquire a hobby; maybe something like gardening where you get physically tired; (2) Get a pet (from the SPCA, where you only pay for the pet's shots). I know many people who derive much pleasure and companionship from a little dog or cat. Taking care of their pet takes their mind off themselves as they consider their pet's needs. However, if you struggle with depression, you may need to talk with your doctor for his recommendation.

Reading is my favorite pastime. In particular, reading the scriptures never fails to encourage me. Reading in the Psalms, for example, inspires me, "I will lift up mine eyes unto the hills from whence comes my help. My help comes from the Lord, which made heaven and earth. He will not suffer thy foot to be moved: he that keeps thee will not slumber...the Lord is thy keeper... the Lord shall preserve thee from all evil: he shall preserve thy soul. The Lord shall preserve thy going out and thy coming in from this time forth, and even for evermore" (Psalm 121, KJV). My heart rejoices during these times of reading because I know the Lord cares for me—the greatest blessing of all.

Henry David Thoreau, who wrote much about returning to a simpler life, had this to say about solitude: "I never found the companion that was so companionable as solitude. We are for the most part more lonely when we go abroad among men than when we stay in our own chambers. A man thinking or working is always alone, let him be where he will."

Henry David Thoreau, "Solitude"
(1817-1862)

[5]*Helen Keller: Her Life in Pictures.* George Sullivan. Scholastic Nonfiction, Inc., NY, NY, 2007; pp. [5a]22, [5b]30, [5c]26.

CHAPTER FIVE

THE CHALLENGES OF ADVERSITY

"I can't go on—this trial is too difficult!"

"Sweet are the uses of adversity,
Which, like the toad, ugly and venomous,
Wears yet a precious jewel in his head.
And this our life, exempt from public haunt,
Finds tongues in trees, books in the running brooks,
Sermons in stones, and good in everything."
William Shakespeare (1564-1616)

Rare is the life that doesn't encounter adversity in one form or another. The shock of something unexpected happening can throw us into a tailspin: a freak accident, maybe resulting in the death of a friend or loved one, the diagnosis of a terminal illness, a large, unexpected bill that you can't pay—even a husband or wife stating, "I don't love you anymore—I'm leaving!" Each of these events can cause a free fall in your life.

Sometimes, even bad news or a cutting remark from someone close to you, can result in a reaction of alarm, setting off your adrenaline. That's one reason I try hard to turn off bad news—even on TV. Such news tends to depress me, and usually I can't do anything about it. I can always pray about a situation and the people involved, so that's what I try to do.

Another way I combat letting things in general pull my spirits down is to avoid negative people. Some people always see the glass half empty instead of half full. Believe me, neither your life nor mine will be enriched by associating with such people. On the other hand, you can always find people who have a cheerful, happy outlook on life despite their circumstances. These people have looked for and found a way through their circumstances.

When I worked for the Chicago Red Cross as a nineteen-year-old swimming instructor several years ago, I taught swimming to several paraplegic veterans at one pool. They were paralyzed from the waist down so they couldn't use their legs. But they had powerful, well-developed chest and arm muscles. What always impressed me about these men, though, was their optimistic outlook on life. Maybe some of them hoped for a cure but the majority were thankful for the use of their arms and what they could do. Their cheerful, outgoing spirits were contagious and I enjoyed being around them.

Dave Thomas, Founder of Wendy's Restaurants (1932-2002)

Someone who illustrates how to overcome adversity is Dave Thomas, the founder of Wendy's Restaurants. Born in 1932 in Atlantic City, New Jersey, Dave himself would say he was nobody special. An illegitimate child, he never knew his birth parents. Then, when he was five years old, his adoptive mother, Auleva, contracted rheumatic fever and died a short time later.

In the hospital, he remembered "How white everything was: her face, the sheets, the floor, the nurses;" but he remembered, too, "Everything was so colorful at the funeral home, and there were flowers and people everywhere."[6] His mother's death and its aftermath

confused the young boy. Only his adoptive grandmother, Minnie Sinclair, tried to explain what had happened to him. She said his mother had gone to heaven
and was watching over him.

Dave loved being at Minnie's Michigan home in
the summertime. She and young Dave had a close relationship. In fact, she had the strongest influence on the
young boy until he was eight or nine years old. Dave
remembers Minnie as being strong willed, not having a
lot but making the most of what she had. After her husband was killed while working on the railroad, Minnie
took whatever work she could find so she could support her four children. She always told David, "Hard
work is good for the soul, and it keeps you from feeling
sorry for yourself because you don't have time."[6a]

Grandma Sinclair had a small farm and raised
chickens and hogs and grew vegetables; she also
worked part-time at Solstrum's, a local restaurant.
When Dave came to visit in the summer, she told him,
"I have to work all week in my garden and around the
house, but once Saturday comes, it will be our special
day together. Then, Sunday is our day with the Lord."[6b]

On Saturday, the two rode to downtown Kalama-
zoo in Minnie's Model A Ford. They first stopped at
the five and dime store, Dave's favorite place. He especially liked the store's shiny, bright-red store sign
that covered nearly the entire length of the building.
The young boy liked nearly everything in the store,
too. He enjoyed watching people move from counter
to counter sifting through stacks of merchandise from
"Big Ben alarm clocks and Lily of the Valley toilet water, Baby Ruth bars and Cannon Towels, Fruit of the
Loom shorts and Lava Soap. It was all there."[6c] After
glancing over merchandise at the store, Dave and his
grandmother had lunch at the counter where they sat
in swivel seats. Usually, he'd order a barbecue sand-
wich or a sloppy Joe.

Their next stop would be the toy counter where the young boy bought a small toy from the money Grandma Minnie gave him. The last stop was the candy counter where his grandmother would wink at him, and say, "The usual, David?" He just "winked" back at her in reply while she ordered bridge mix and orange slices for both of them.[6d]

Dave's times with his adoptive father, Rex Thomas, were different. His father went through a succession of marriages, each new wife finding fault with the young boy. After one of the wives, Marie, left, Dave and his father started eating out a lot. Again, the young boy was impressed with the various restaurants and thought they were organized and exciting places. By the age of nine, Dave had become an expert on restaurants. He knew what customers wanted and expected. He also understood the kind of service and quality that was acceptable. He had already determined in his mind that he would own a restaurant when he grew up.

Even at the young ages of ten and eleven, Dave worked at various places such as a Walgreen's soda fountain job. When he was fired from that job and his father got angry, he quickly found another job at the Regas Restaurant in downtown Knoxville, Tennessee. So, at just twelve years of age, Dave began to put in twelve-hour days behind the restaurant counter. The young boy liked his new employers, Frank and George Regas, and they treated him like family. When Dave's family moved to Fort Wayne, Indiana in 1947, they moved into a trailer; but Dave missed living on his own. So he located a new job at the Hobby House Restaurant where he worked on the fountain. The owner of the Hobby House was Phil Clauss. He took Dave "under his wing," and encouraged him at every opportunity.

A short time later, Mr. Thomas told his son he was moving again; but Dave made up his mind to stay in Fort Wayne. He considered the Clauss family his own family so he decided not to move with his dad and his new wife. He told his dad at that time, though, "Someday you'll be proud of me. I'm going to have my own restaurant, and I'm going to be a success." His dad replied, "I hope you're right, son. Good luck to you." [6e] Dave didn't see his father for three years after that although they talked on the phone once or twice and exchanged Christmas cards. A little later, Dave quit school while he was in the tenth grade. He wasn't learning what he wanted to learn about the restaurant business. In 1950, with the onset of war in Korea, Dave joined the army where he worked as a cook. Many of the cooking innovations he used in the army were solutions he had found to earlier problems. Even applying a fresh coat of paint to the mess hall to improve the soldiers' morale was something he learned before he joined the army.

Out of the army in 1953 where he had profited much from his culinary job, Dave came back to the Hobby House. His former boss, Phil Clauss was glad to see him, offering him his old job back. Almost his first day back at the restaurant, he met an attractive 18-year-old waitress named Lorraine Buskirk. They began to date and in 1954, they were married.

When Colonel Harland Sanders entered Dave's life, however, his life went into orbit. Phil Clauss ended up putting Kentucky Fried Chicken in both his restaurants and emphasizing the "take out" aspect of the chicken. Sales began to soar, and soon, Dave found himself managing one of the Hobby House Restaurants—all because of Colonel Sanders' Kentucky Fried Chicken. Dave and the Colonel became good friends, and Dave learned much from him—especially ideas like creating an image and philosophy for himself. He also learned the importance of having an ultra-clean restaurant and serving top-notch products. The Colonel had established his own particular image with his white suit, string tie, white goatee and gold-tipped cane.

In 1958, Dave got the big break he'd hoped for. He went to Columbus, Ohio to manage four failing Kentucky Fried Chicken franchises. They were Hobby House franchises but selling KFC exclusively. Some of the things Dave did to make the restaurants successful were 1) Removed all menu items except chicken and the dishes that went with it, 2) Fired all four managers 3) Applied fresh paint to each place to improve morale as well as making each store look attractive 4) Promoted through advertising—swapping chicken for advertising!

In time, he was able to turn the four restaurants around and make much money in the process. Later Kentucky Fried Chicken bought back Dave's four restaurants. The sale netted him and Phil Clauss 1.7 million dollars in KFC stock. Dave's percentage of the sale was 41 percent, making him a millionaire. That was enough for him to go into the hamburger business, which he did a year or two later. He applied the same principles at the age of 37 to having the best possible restaurant serving hamburgers. He also decided to call his restaurant "Wendy's" after his youngest daughter.

So, on November 15, 1969, Dave opened the first Wendy's in Columbus, Ohio. The restaurant caught on right away as Dave implemented all the ideas he had learned working with different restaurants from the time he was twelve. Before long, Wendy's hamburgers took off as Dave opened one store after another. There are now thousands of Wendy's restaurants worldwide. As Burt Reynolds commented about him, "Dave Thomas exemplifies the true American. The odds were against him from the start and he maintained his goal. His life has become an example for all of us. Dave Thomas, a true inspiration."[6f]

The Fire

"Did you know your house burned to the ground a little while ago?" The dark-haired woman shrieked at me as I stood opening my dark-green locker in the school hallway. As she finished saying that, I burst into tears, grabbed my light-weight tan coat, slammed the locker shut, and started running for home as fast as I could all the while crying convulsively.

About 15 minutes later, I reached my home and to my delight, the white frame house was still there. My mother came to meet me as I opened the back door. "Mom, what's happened?" I asked. My mother, usually composed in crisis times, said, "Yes, we had a fire in the downstairs' bedroom and the fire trucks just left. But everything is under control now." I walked quickly to the bedroom to view the charred remains: the fire had destroyed the furniture, and the room was totally gutted. But the fire was confined to the bedroom for which we were thankful.

Then I saw the lovely pink dress with pearl buttons down the front hanging on a pole that stretched between the two parlors. *Oh, good,* I thought. *My dress is fine.* I planned to wear the dress to sing between acts of the Junior Class Play in a few days. When I went over to remove the dress, however, it fell apart from the smoke damage. My heart sank, and I felt terrible. *What would I wear to sing in?* My tears started up all over again.

As it turned out, some good came from this tragedy to my family. A kind teacher with whom I was close, offered to have me choose a new dress. Then a local civic club in my little town, paid for a beautiful gray winter coat I had put on lay-a-way and was diligently paying money on each week. Many people reached out to my family in different ways offering food, support, and encouragement.

Singing my solo a week or so later in a lovely, deep-blue dress, I felt almost as confident as I would have in the pink one. And one of the lessons I realized from this tragedy is that people often surprise us with their caring and with their kindness. But sometimes it takes a tragedy to bring out their better qualities.

"Defeat may serve as well as victory
To shake the soul and let the glory out.
When the great oak is straining in the wind,
the boughs drink in new beauty and the trunk
sends down a deeper root on the windward side.
Only the soul that knows the mighty grief
Can know the mighty rapture. Sorrows come
to stretch out spaces in the heart for joy."
Edwin Markham (1852-1940)

"If you fall to pieces in a crisis, there wasn't much to you in the first place."
Proverbs 24:14, (*The Message Bible*)

Some of the "sweet uses of adversity" Shakespeare speaks of can be glimpsed in Romans 5:3-6:

"This doesn't mean, of course, that we have only a hope of future joys—we can be full of joy here and now even in our trials and troubles. Taken in the right spirit these very things will give us patient endurance; this in turn will develop a mature character, and a character of this sort produces a steady hope, a hope that will never disappoint us. Already we have some experience of the love of God flooding through our hearts by the Holy Spirit given to us"   Romans 5:3-6
J.B. Phillips, *The New Testament in Modern English*

[6]*Dave's Way*, R. David Thomas. G. P. Putnam's Sons. New York, N.Y. pp.19, [6a]20, [6b]21, [6c]21, [6d]21, [6e]48, [6f]Preface.

CHAPTER SIX

SEEKING SUPPORT

"I don't need anyone's help"

"Nothing is there more friendly to a man than a friend in need."

Titus Maccius Plautus (254-184 B.C.)

Annie Sullivan, Helen Keller's Teacher (1866-1936)

Annie Sullivan was Irish through and through with a fiery temper to match her nationality. Born on April 14, 1866, in a small village in Western Massachusetts called Feeding Hills, Annie Sullivan knew only crushing poverty from her earliest days. Her father, Thomas Sullivan, was an unskilled, illiterate laborer. Thomas and his wife, Alice, immigrated to America in the 19th century in search of a better land. He was also an alcoholic with an explosive temper who beat five-year-old Annie severely; her mother tried to hide Annie from him. On Thomas's good days, however, he sang Irish songs and told Annie stories of the legendary "Little People" and fairy folk back in Ireland.

When Annie was around five years old, her eyes began to trouble her. They became red and swollen and clouded over, and they felt scratchy and sore. Annie recalls someone saying to her at that time, "She would be so pretty if it were not for her eyes."[7] Her eye problem was later diagnosed as trachoma, a contagious eye disease. Gradually, the disease began to destroy her vision.

At the age of eight, Annie's mother died from tuberculosis, leaving her father with three children: Annie, the oldest, five-year-old Jimmie, who had a crippling lump on his hip from tuberculosis, and Mary a strong, healthy toddler. A short time later, Thomas abandoned his children, leaving them for relatives to raise. Little Mary was soon taken in by an aunt, but no one wanted half-blind Annie and little, crippled Jimmie. So Annie and Jimmie were sent to live in the state-run "poor house" in Tewksbury, Massachusetts. The Tewksbury facility provided shelter and care for poor and needy people who had nowhere else to go.

The institution lacked any special place for orphaned children, and Annie and Jimmie spent their first night there in the "dead house," a room where the attendants prepared dead bodies for burial. Sadly, the Tewksbury facility enhanced the possibility of death with its run-down, filthy, and overcrowded conditions. In addition, many of the inmates were diseased, mentally ill, or both. Some had been drunks or criminals and violent. None were fit company for children.

In spite of their circumstances, Annie and Jimmie did the best they could, given their surroundings. They even made a playroom out of the rat-infested area. But Jimmie lived only three months after they arrived at Tewksbury. Annie remembered about that time, "Suddenly I missed Jimmie's bed. The black, empty space where it had been filled me with wild fear."[7a]

Annie lived inside the Tewksbury gates for four more years after Jimmie's death. She learned how to take care of herself and avoid the troublemakers. She survived largely because she was interested in everything, however indecent or cruel.

She had her eyes operated on twice, but her vision continued to decline. All she could see were "bright colors dancing in a perpetual and bewildering procession."[7b] About this time, one of the other inmates told Annie about schools for blind children. So, with Irish determination, Annie made up her mind that one day, she would go to school.

At the age of 14, Annie got her chance. She learned that a group of inspectors, led by a Mr. Sanborn, were coming to Tewksbury to investigate its wretched condition. When the inspectors arrived, Annie threw herself into their midst, crying, "Mr. Sanborn, Mr. Sanborn, I want to go to school!"[7c]

Her wish was granted, and she transferred shortly to the Perkins Institution for the blind in Boston, Massachusetts. But the Perkins Institution, with its quiet, polite ways was very different from rough and tumble Tewksbury. Annie felt like a round peg in a square hole at Perkins. She was large for her age, yet childlike in many ways, "and utterly unacquainted with the usages of civilized people."[7d]

Most of the students came from middle-class or well-to-do backgrounds, but Annie didn't even own a nightgown or a hairbrush when she arrived. She could neither read nor write and didn't even know her own birthday. Because of her Irish accent, rough manners, and general ignorance, many of the students and some of the teachers, ridiculed her. She even missed Tewksbury!

In spite of all her humiliation, Annie's teachers soon realized she possessed a superior intelligence. She learned the alphabet using raised letter type; she learned Braille quickly, too. Annie also began to make friends, including a friend named Laura Bridgman, a deaf and blind student who had learned to read and write. Her teacher, Dr. Samuel Howe, had developed a new method of communication with her referred to as the manual alphabet. Dr. Howe would give Laura an object such as a spoon with its name printed on it in raised letters. The "talker" then used the finger movements to communicate with the "listener" the name of the object. Annie learned the finger alphabet so she could talk with Laura Bridgman.

While at Perkins, Annie had two more operations on her eyes that gave her enough restored vision so she could read printed materials. Afterward, she devoured book after book, though her eyes tired easily.

By the time she graduated from Perkins on June 1, 1886, Annie Sullivan had risen to the top of her graduating class and gave the valedictory address to her class. She told her classmates, "We…have the power of controlling the course of our lives. We can educate ourselves; we can by thought and perseverance, develop all the powers and capacities entrusted to us."[7e]

During the summer, however, Annie worried about earning a living. But one day a letter arrived from Michael Anagnos, the Perkins' Director. He had received a note from an Arthur Keller in Alabama asking for someone to teach his seven-year-old deaf, blind, and mute daughter, Helen. Mr. Anagnos wondered if Annie would be interested. Of course, she was, and even said about her going to Alabama to teach Helen Keller, "I know that the education of this child will be the distinguishing event of my life, if I have the brains and perseverance to accomplish it."[7f]

Annie Sullivan went on to teach Helen Keller and "unlock" her bright mind; she also spent the rest of her life with Helen as her teacher-companion. As the two of them traveled the world becoming renowned in places like Japan and India, Annie realized that her coming to teach Helen Keller was, indeed, "The distinguishing event of her life," all because she cried out for help at Tewksbury, saying, "I want to go to school!"

"Not in the clamor of the crowded street,
Not in the shouts and plaudits of the throng,
But in ourselves are triumph and defeat."

Henry Wadsworth Longfellow (1807-1882)

The Satin Dress

Living in Florida, I began to prepare for a Christmas visit to my husband's home state of Connecticut. I was caught up with cutting out and sewing a gold satin dress. But I struggled with keeping the satin material from moving long enough to cut out the pattern. The satin material would slip and slide until I despaired of ever getting the dress cut out properly.

In the midst of my dilemma, I heard a knock at the front door. It was my cheerful, older neighbor, Clara, taking her daily walk. She wore her customary, navy Bermuda shorts that displayed her tanned, muscular legs. Clara's husband had Parkinson's disease and formerly played the violin. Now, because of his shaking, he could no longer finger and play the violin—a great frustration to both Clara and her husband.

When Clara realized what I was doing, she shook her short-cropped gray hair and said, "Bonnie, let me show you one way to keep the fabric still so you can pin the pattern on it and cut it out." With that, Clara put the reverse side of the satin material on top. Because it wasn't shiny, the pins were easily inserted into it.

Later, I finished sewing the dress and wore it to a special holiday function in Connecticut. A number of people even complimented me telling me what an attractive dress it was. I knew I owed a great debt to my kind neighbor and friend in Florida for her "helping hand." And I was grateful to her for my lovely, gold satin dress.

A Neighbor Who Needed Help

"There was once a man traveling from Jerusalem to Jericho. On the way he was attacked by robbers. They took his clothes, beat him up, and went off, leaving him half-dead. Luckily a priest was on his way down the same road, but when he saw him he angled across to the other side. Then a Levite religious man showed up; he also avoided the injured man.

A Samaritan traveling the road came on him. When he saw the man's condition, his heart went out to him. He gave him first aid, disinfecting and bandaging his wounds. Then he lifted him onto his donkey, led him to an inn, and made him comfortable. In the morning, he took out two silver coins and gave them to the innkeeper saying, 'Take good care of him. If it costs any more, put it on my bill—I'll pay you on my way back.'"

Luke 10:30-35
(*The Message Bible*)

"The greatest love is shown when a man lays down his life for his friends."

John 15:13, (TLB)

[7]*Helen's Eyes: A Photo biography of Annie Sullivan, Helen Keller's Teacher.* Marfe Ferguson Delano, National Geographic, 2008. (pp.10, [7a]12, [7b]12, [7c]13, [7d]13, [7e]19, [7f]Frontspiece).

CHAPTER SEVEN

THE DIFFICULTIES WITH PRIDE AND REPUTATION

"What will I do when others find out what has happened?"

"He that is down need fear no fall,
He that is low, no pride."
Shepherd Boy's Song
John Bunyan (1628-1688)

Acquiring A Doubtful Reputation

When I was a naïve thirteen-year-old high school freshman, like many adolescents, I wanted to be well liked. Some of my good friends were from fine families, and I enjoyed being with them. But there was one girl who was a couple of years older than me who fascinated me. She had gorgeous blonde hair, an attractive figure, a great personality and was always fun to be with.

As time passed, however, I noticed that she really didn't care, especially when it came to boys, who she associated with. One night, after eating burgers at a local hangout, she said, "Bonnie, come go with Bob and me. There's someone you can date, too." I held back from going with this girl and her friends that night because rumors circulated as to what had happened to her. I also noticed that some of my other friends were avoiding me. These things combined to "wake me up," so I stopped associating with the girl with the dubious reputation.

I learned from this experience that it matters who your friends are. Even if you're not exactly like they are, other people judge you according to the people with whom you associate. An interesting verse in the Bible sums up the situation: "Do not be misled: Bad company corrupts good character" (1 Corinthians 15:33, NIV). At a tender age, I learned a worthwhile lesson through this experience.

This Day is Mine to Mar or Make

"This day is mine to mar or make,
God keep me strong and true,
Let me no erring by-path take,
No doubtful action do.

Grant me when the setting sun
This fleeting day shall end,
I may rejoice o'er something done,
Be richer by a friend.

Let all I meet along the way
Speak well of me tonight.
I would not have the humblest say
I'd hurt him by a slight.

Let there be something true and fine
When night slips down to tell
That I have lived this day of mine
Not selfishly but well."

Anonymous

Corrie Ten Boom, Concentration Camp Survivor (1892-1983)

Haarlem, Holland in the 1930's seems an unlikely place of preparation for someone who would bear much tragedy for the Christian faith. Yet Cornelia (Corrie) Ten Boom, the future woman of faith, was born to a watchmaker, Casper Ten Boom, and his wife on April 15, 1892.

Corrie's childhood and adolescent years were happy, secure ones with her father reading from the big, brass-hinged Bible and having daily prayers. Life revolved around the family business, the clock shop, where Casper and his apprentices made and fixed watches and clocks. The Ten Boom house and shop in Haarlem had been in the family for generations. The old house, which was one room wide and two rooms deep, was really two houses tacked together in a long-ago time.

Extended family members had lived in the house, too, but now, although the three aunts were deceased, the current occupants thought of them as still with them. The present family members besides Corrie, consisted of Betsie (Corrie's sister) and Caspar, her father. Corrie's sister, Nollie, and brother, Willem, a minister brother, had married and had families of their own. Mama Ten Boom had died several years earlier, in 1921. But they still sensed Mama's presence in this odd little house.

Of course, in addition to the Ten Boom house's present occupants, Corrie's father always insisted on taking in anyone who came to his door in need. He was especially fond of children and ended up providing for eleven foster children in the Ten Boom house.

The days at the watch shop proceeded uneventfully enough with a formerly itinerant clock minder, Christoffels, who helped Caspar, and Toos, the bookkeeper. Corrie liked the way her father "ticked" as he wore three and four watches at a time to regulate them.

Now, in 1937, much was changing not only in Holland, but also in neighboring Germany. The Ten Booms received word regularly about Jewish clock shops in Germany being closed and going out of business. Their owners often mysteriously disappeared. Corrie's brother, Willem, a minister in Holland, had even built a home for elderly Jews in Holland; but actually, it was a home for people of all faiths.

From the time he attended university in Germany and wrote his doctoral thesis, Willem could see horrible things beginning to take place in Germany such as the disregard for human life. When Willem attended his father's clock shop's 100th birthday party in January 1937, he brought a guest with him, a Herr Gutlieber, a Jewish man from Germany. The man's face had been burned by teenagers in Munich, Germany as he attempted to leave the country, which he finally did—hiding in a milk truck. The teenagers had set fire to his beard leaving an open, gaping wound.

Corrie, too, as she reflected on the 100th birthday party's events considered childhood scenes from the past and realized that often "Such memories are the key not to the past but to the future...the experiences of our lives, when we let God use them, become the mysterious and perfect preparation for the work He will give us to do."[8] Her humdrum life at that time hardly indicated any new future for which to prepare.

Events moved swiftly for Corrie and her family from that day in 1937 as more and more Jewish people, in particular, sought refuge not only at Willem's place, but at the clock shop and the curious little house called the "Beje." Soon, Corrie's brother, Willem, who also harbored people (mostly Jews) who came to him, helped her with making a "secret room" at the house in which people could hide. He also helped her obtain the necessary "ration" cards for each individual.

As the war continued, the Ten Boom house overflowed with people seeking refuge. But one day, on February 28, 1944, the house and shop were raided by the Nazis, and Corrie, Betsie, and their father were arrested and taken to Scheveningen, a concentration camp in Germany. In the camp, Corrie, Betsie, and the other women prisoners were subjected to much humiliation as they stood naked before the Nazi men on different occasions. During the long days, they were assigned to heavy manual labor like shoveling and working with heavy equipment. Betsie's health, never good, was challenged by these times.

Corrie and Betsie were transferred from one cell to another where they encountered lice, then fleas in the straw used for bedding. But Corrie had also managed to smuggle a Bible into prison with her. Miraculously, the guards never saw it so Corrie and Betsie conducted Bible studies and prayer in their cells on a regular basis. These meetings were well attended by the prisoners and offered some hope for their bleak existence.

Corrie even had a chance to share something of the Bible with a Nazi officer, a Lieutenant Rahms, in the prison. The second time he interrogated her about her involvement in hiding Jews at her home in Holland, the officer said, "I could not sleep last night, thinking about that Book [the Bible] where you read such different ideas. What else does it say?"[8a]

Corrie thought for a moment then replied, "It says that a Light has come into this world, so that we need no longer walk in the dark. Is there darkness in your life, Lieutenant?"[8b]

"There is great darkness; I cannot bear the work I do here," he answered.[8c]

Corrie answered thoughtfully after the officer spoke of his family and his concern for them, "There

is One who has them always in His sight, Lieutenant
Rahms. Jesus is the Light the Bible shows to me, the
Light that can shine even in such darkness as yours."[8d]

Sometime later, as Betsie and Corrie talked, Betsie spoke of a man named Jan Vogel, a Dutchman
who worked for the Gestapo. He was the person who
turned in Corrie's brother, Willem, and her father. Corrie sensed an immense hatred rise up within her toward this man. But she was puzzled by her sister's attitude toward Jan Vogel. After a sleepless night of feeling
such hatred and rage toward Vogel, Corrie asked Betsie
about her feeling toward the man who had betrayed
their family. Betsie said, "Oh, yes, Corrie! I've felt for
him ever since I knew what had happened. I pray for
him whenever his name comes into my mind. How
dreadfully he must be suffering!"[8e]

Corrie felt smitten by Betsie's words and scarcely
thought she knew this sister of hers. She forgave such
terrible wrongs so easily. But Betsie's forgiving attitude
toward Jan Vogel made Corrie feel that she, herself,
was as guilty as Vogel. She had such intense hatred in
her heart toward him. What did the Bible teach about
love? Corrie sensed that she had murdered Vogel in her
heart and with her tongue.

Then she prayed into the lumpy ticking of the bed,
"I forgive Jan Vogel as I pray you will forgive me. I
have done him great damage. Bless him now, and his
family."[8f] For the first night in a long time, Corrie slept
dreamlessly and peacefully until the morning whistle
blew.

A short time later, everyone in the prison barracks
was rounded up and put on a freight train headed for
the infamous prison called "Ravensbruck," deep in
the heart of Germany. The people were jam-packed in
the freight car with no room to move or do anything
else. After three days and nights the car arrived at Ravensbruck, located near Berlin. Sadly, Betsie died at

Ravensbruck due to ill treatment and malnutrition on December 16, 1944.

A scarce ten days after Betsie's death, Corrie was freed from the prison, and by January 1, 1945, she arrived back in Holland. After spending some time in mental and physical rehabilitation, Corrie began to travel and speak about her experiences. She became well known as she traveled to many lands where God used her greatly to speak on love and forgiveness. Betsie had always emphasized that "There is no pit so deep but God's love is deeper still," and Corrie wanted to prove that in her own life.

Because Corrie was willing to humble herself and forgive even Jan Vogel and anyone else who had wronged her, she received God's "Seal of Approval" on herself and her ministry. In spite of tremendous odds, Corrie Ten Boom forsook pride and reputation and not only survived her concentration camp ordeal, but the experience provided her with her life's work and ministry as she traveled worldwide telling her story.

"Pride goes before destruction, a haughty spirit before a fall."

(Proverbs 16:18, NIV)

"God gives special blessings to those who are humble, but sets Himself against those who are proud. If you will humble yourselves under the mighty hand of God, in his good time he will lift you up."

(1 Peter 5-6, TLB)

[8]*The Hiding Place*, 35th Anniversary Edition, Corrie Ten Boom (with John and Elizabeth Sherrill), Chosen Books. Grand Rapids, MI, 1971, 1984: pp. 31, [8a]173, [8b]174, [8c]174, [8d]192, [8e]192, [8f]192-193

Chapter Eight

Facing Your Aging Process

"I'm too old to deal with this!"

"Grow old along with me!
The best is yet to be,
The last of life, for which the first was made:
Our times are in his hand
Who saith, 'A whole is planned,
Youth shows but half; trust God: see all nor be
afraid!'"

"Rabbi Ben Ezra," Stanza One
Robert Browning (1812-1869)

Lee Iacocca, Proving the Wisdom of Age (1924-?)

"On July 13, 1978, I was fired. I had been president of Ford for eight years and a Ford employee for thirty-two. I had never worked anywhere else. And now, suddenly, I was out of a job. It was gut wrenching."[9]

Officially, Lee's term as president was to expire on October 15, his fifty-fourth birthday. Lee, and his secretary, Dorothy Carr, met in his new "office," which was a far cry from his presidential suite at Ford with all its accouterments, including private bathroom and even his own living quarters. White-coated waiters were at his beck and call all day long. But now, Lee sat in a tiny cubicle located inside an old, decaying warehouse with cracked linoleum floors. His secretary was waiting for him with two chipped plastic coffee cups and tears in her eyes. When the incongruity of his surroundings sunk in and as he assessed his situation, Lee promptly picked up his few belongings and left—never to return.

In spite of his humiliation over the firing, Lee's next question was, "What do I do now?" He faced a fork in life's road and had to do something to overcome the public disgrace over his firing. Lee's wife, Mary, reminded him, "Don't get mad, get even"[9a] That's when Lee determined to go with Chrysler Motor Co. as their new president. At that time Chrysler was skirting bankruptcy, so Lee had his hands full.

Lee Iacocca came from hard-working Italian immigrant parents, Nicola and Antoinette Iacocca. His father had come to America at the age of twelve in 1902. Some years later he met and married Antoinette. Lido, or Lee (the Americanization of his name), their firstborn, arrived on October 15, 1924.

As he grew up, Lee was close to his father who loved to brag about his son. Whether Lee won a spelling contest in elementary school or later, if he brought out a new car at Ford, his father showed his immense pride in his son by telling all his friends about his accomplishments.

Although his father operated a number of businesses, at the time of Lee's birth he owned a hot-dog restaurant called the "Orpheum Weiner House." The Weiner House hadn't been difficult to get into. All he needed were a grill, a bun warmer, and stools for the customers to sit on. The low-cost outlay shows two principles of his father's: "Never get into a capital intensive business because the bankers will end up owning you... and when times are tough, be in the food business...no matter how bad things get, people still have to eat"[9b]

Lee had a happy childhood with a close, loving family relationship with his father, mother, and sister,

Delma, in Allentown, Pennsylvania. And, although his father refused to let him own a bike because of his own mishap on a Harley-Davidson, Lee was the first kid in Allentown to drive a car when he turned sixteen.

As a teenager, Lee had a weekend job in a fruit market owned by a Greek named Jimmy Kristis. Lee got up before dawn to go to the produce market, then brought the produce back. He earned $2 a day plus all the fruit and vegetables he could carry home after working sixteen hours a day.

During the Depression times in the 1920's, Lee's family struggled to make ends meet; in fact, the family came close to losing their home. Lee recalls the family praying a lot during this time and going to Mass every Sunday and taking Holy Communion every week or two. Even though times were hard, Lee's family had fun, too. On Sunday evenings, the family gathered around the Philco radio and listened to Edgar Bergen and Charlie McCarthy and "Inner Sanctum."

Because of the effects of the Depression on the Iacoccas, Lee's father insisted he attend college in order to understand how to avoid losing everything in another depression. Prior to attending college, Lee excelled in high school with straight A's in math, being the top Latin student, and was active in Drama Club and the debating society. He even played a tenor saxophone as his token to the "big-band" era .

By the time he enrolled in Lehigh University in Bethlehem, Pennsylvania, the Japanese had attacked Pearl Harbor. Lee wanted to sign up for the armed services, but because he'd had rheumatic fever when he was younger, the army wouldn't take him. But he entered college with an engineering degree in mind. He took classes six days a week, including a Saturday class at 8:00 a.m. in statistics. He got an "A" in the class, perhaps just because he persevered while other classmates slept in.

Some of the important lessons he learned in college (and some before) were establishing priorities and using his time wisely. He had already learned when he was younger to do his homework first, then go play. Rarely did Lee violate this principle—and it stood him well the rest of his life.

Lee had been chosen to work for Ford Motor Company his senior year after he graduated. But before he started with Ford, he learned of a graduate fellowship at Princeton. The grant covered tuition, books, and even spending money. His contact at Ford, a Mr. McCormick-Goodheart, advised him to attend Princeton—Ford would hold his slot open.

He was finally ready to join Ford after a productive year at Princeton in August 1946. His years at Ford proved to be encouraging ones as he worked his way up the corporate ladder. Many of the courses he'd had at Princeton, such as psychology classes, served him well as he learned to evaluate people in the business world. He did switch his interests at Ford from engineering to sales, though, which better suited his abilities and interests. In time, Lee came under the influence of Charlie Beacham, whom he considered his mentor. Charlie once told him, "Always remember that everybody makes mistakes, but most people don't own up to them. Most people try to blame someone else—their wife, kids, etc. So, if you screw up, don't give me any excuses—go look at yourself in the mirror. Then come see me."[9c]

In 1970, Lee was appointed to the presidency of Ford Motor Company where he remained for eight years. He lost his position possibly because of infighting or jealousy. At any rate, he had to decide what to do the rest of his life at age 54, not an easy task. He did have some intriguing job offers but decided to go with Chrysler as their new president. Unfortunately, Chrysler skirted bankruptcy for some time and the U.S. government had to bail out the company. But the company paid the loan back on time—to the tune of billions of dollars.

Lee (Lido) Iacocca is well known today for his quick thinking and maneuvering at Chrysler to get the company back on solid footing. He stayed with Chrysler until his retirement in 1992 when he left the now thriving company. He now spends his days at age 87 with his two daughters, Kathi and Lia, speaking at business schools, and enjoying time off to enjoy recreational pursuits.

Lee Iacocca has achieved much, even at an age when many people retire. He would be the first to admit that some of his most productive years happened at Chrysler when he was in his mid fifties, even to his seventies. If he had retired at 54 after leaving Ford, his mature years of wisdom would never have been used—and Chrysler probably would never have been bailed out.

Too Young

After signing up to take a course on "Becoming a Water Safety Instructor," I was so excited. Now I could approach the YWCA to teach swimming in one of their summer camps.

The course, offered by the small college I attended, would last roughly six weeks of intensive training. I was a good swimmer, and my instructor often used me to demonstrate new swimming techniques to the class. Everything went smoothly in the course until the final day for the life-saving exam. I had been quite sick with a virus and it had weakened me. But I had to take the test or forget the whole course until it would be offered again. So, I chose to take the test.

My "guinea pig," however, was a tall, husky farm girl who weighed at least 200 or more pounds. She fought and fought me in the water, flailing her arms and kicking with her legs; all I could think of was, "I've got to rescue her so I can pass the test and teach at a YWCA camp!" After struggling with her for what seemed like an hour, I finally succeeded in rescuing her from drowning. Exhausted, I was so relieved and thought, "Thank goodness, now I'll have my water-safety instructor certificate to teach!"

Later, after sending my application to the "Y" headquarters, I was turned down because of my age. Their instructors had to be 21. Although I was terribly disappointed, I went to Chicago that summer and ended up working for the Red Cross teaching swimming at many different pools around the city. The Red Cross even offered me an opportunity to become a Junior Director for their organization. So, although I was too young for the "Y" job, working for the Red Cross turned out to be a great opportunity for me even though I chose not to become a Junior director.

The Truth about Age

Someone has said, "Age is just a number," and indeed it is. If you're mentally and physically sound and want to pursue a certain direction, whatever your age, do it!

We've given a few examples in this book of people who are over a certain age yet have succeeded in a particular field. Keep your mind open to the possibilities of what you can accomplish if you discount the age factor. Remember, you're as old or as young as you think you are!

"You are old, Father William," the young man said,
"And your hair has become very white; and yet you incessantly stand on your head; do you think, at your age, it is right?"   Lewis Carroll (1832-1898)

Alice in *Alice in Wonderland*, Ch. 5
[9]*Iacocca, Lee Iacocca* (with William Novak), G.K. Hall & Co., Boston, 1985, pp. Xi, Xv, [9a]7, [9b]8, [9c]58.

CHAPTER NINE

COPING WITH HEALTH PROBLEMS

"My Health is Failing"

"For some patients, though conscious that their condition is perilous, recover their health simply through their contentment with the goodness of the Physician."
Hippocrates (460-377 B.C.)

"A cheerful heart {spirit} is good medicine, But a crushed spirit dries up the bones."
Proverbs 17:22, NIV

Lou Gehrig, New York Yankees' First Baseman (1903-1941)

The New York Yankees first baseman, Lou Gehrig, had an amazing record with the ball club. For the fourteen years he played with them, he never missed a single game, earning him the nickname "Iron Horse." His stamina with the team also helped him play 2,130 consecutive games. Lou considered himself a very lucky man despite the fact he was diagnosed with a rare disease and illness of the central nervous system when he was just thirty-six years old.

Lou Gehrig was born in 1903 in the Yorkville section of New York City. In addition to his own immigrant parents, Heinrich and Christina Gehrig, the Yor-kville area was populated with poor immigrants.

Christina Gehrig had ambitious plans for her son; she hoped he would attend college and become an ar-chitect or an engineer. So she wanted him to apply him-self in school and make good grades. Lou earned decent grades and had perfect attendance for eight years of grade school. Lou's mother thought the sports her son played were foolish and a waste of time. Every morn-ing before leaving for school, Lou played baseball, soc-cer, or football. He was a natural athlete and excelled in each sport, but his love was baseball. By the time he entered high school, Lou qualified for his school's base-ball team at Commerce High School in New York City.

His mother tried to keep him as a "Mama's Boy" when he was in high school. She insisted he wear knickers instead of a young man's customary pants. To avoid trouble with his mother, Lou hid a pair of grown-up pants in a container outside the apartment and changed into them before school each day, then put the knickers back on after returning from school.

Lou entered the High School of Commerce at 155 West 65th Street in New York City–a school located a long ride along elevated train tracks from his home. People who knew him at the time used words such as "worried" and "harassed" to describe his facial ex-pressions.[10] But his mother could hardly be blamed for keeping young Lou close to her since she had already lost three of his siblings to early deaths; his father said little on his son's behalf.

Although Lou said in an interview it was his moth-er's decision not to let him play on an athletic team his first year at Commerce, he later said, "I wanted to play ball on the high school team, but lacked the courage to go out for a position until my junior year."[10a] When he finally got involved with high school sports, it was like a tornado exploded. He played soccer, football and baseball: sometimes two sports on the same day. He was weakest at baseball but being six feet tall and weighing 180 pounds, his coach, Harry Kane, couldn't give up on him despite his clumsiness.

The coach started him at first base, then tried him at pitching. He threw the ball hard but lacked control. Of course, he improved with practice. What really excited his coach, however, was his hitting ability. It became evident by the spring of his junior year that Gehrig was one of the most powerful hitters, if not the most powerful hitter to ever emerge from the city's public schools. These powerful hits resulted in Gehrig's numerous home runs. Few men in the big leagues were capable of equaling his feat as he regularly hit balls over fences in high school games.

But his biggest weakness as a hitter was his inability to hit curve balls from left-handed pitchers. So coach Kane, a former big league left-handed pitcher, began pitching curve after curve to his star pupil. After a few weeks of practice, Lou completely overcame his fault.

In spite of spending long hours at baseball practice, Lou also helped his mother, now a cook and house-keeper at Sigma Nu Theta; plus, he did odd jobs like mowing lawns, shoveling snow, and delivering news-papers. Whatever money Gehrig earned, however, was not put toward dressing better. One of his former classmates noted: "No one who went to school with Lou can forget the cold winter days and Lou coming to school wearing khaki shirt, khaki pants and heavy brown shoes, but no overcoat, nor any hat...he was a poor boy."[10b]

The Commerce High baseball team in 1920 was the finest in New York City, and the team headed to Chicago on June 24, a few days after Lou's seventeenth birthday to play a big game in Chicago against the top Chicago team, Lane Technical. The game was played at Cubs Park (later called, Wrigley Field). The Chicago team had been warned about the commerce team, especially about Gehrig: "The Gotham boys have a first baseman, Louis Gehrig, who is called the 'Babe Ruth' of the high schools."[10c] For the next twenty years, Gehrig would be compared to Babe Ruth. If Coach Kane had not made a personal call on the Gehrigs, however, Lou's mother might not have allowed her son to make the trip. She failed to understand that it was a championship game and why he couldn't play ball just as well in New York.

The train trip to Chicago proved life changing for Gehrig as he slept on crisp white sheets, had extra blankets, and uniformed servants to wait on him. Even former President William H. Taft came to their passenger car to wish them well. Once they arrived in Chicago, the young athletes were made over like celebrities. In Chicago, the team climbed into convertibles in an ongoing parade and rode through the city's downtown Loop.

The following day, the game was played at Cubs Park. Gehrig, however, had yet to show himself as much of a ball player: "He grounded back to the pitcher in the second inning, struck out in the fourth with a man on base, then walked again and scored in the sixth. In four at-bats, he put the ball in play only once, and even then hit it feebly."[10d]

Commerce led the game 8-6 in the top of the sixth inning when Gehrig came to bat for the last time. The bases were loaded, with two outs. He stepped confidently into the batter's box, spread his feet in a wide stance, and glared at Lane's new pitcher, Norris Ryrholm. The pitcher wanted to retire Gehrig, but somehow his pitch ended up "floating just where Gehrig liked it, high and inside. Gehrig squeezed the bat and swung, shifting his weight from back to front, channeling the full force of his growing body through his wrists."[10e]

Immediately, Lou knew he'd hit the ball well. He dropped his bat and took off for first base as he kept an eye on the ball zooming higher and higher, over the brick wall in right field and out of sight. Then, it bounced once on Sheffield Avenue and finally rested on the wooden porch of a house across the street. The next day the *New York Daily News* called him the bright star of the inner city high school championship and referred to him as "Babe Gehrig."

On January 27, 1921, Lou graduated from Commerce High School, and a short time later, he enrolled in Columbia University. His mother wanted very much for him to succeed in college and seek a profession. But Lou played on the Columbia University baseball team and again proved to be an outstanding ball player.

On April 26, 1925, a scout for the New York Yankees saw him play, but after Lou hit two long home runs, the Yankees decided to sign him up to play for them. When the Yankees offered him a $1500 bonus to sign plus a good salary, his family reluctantly agreed to the arrangement. His mother thought he was ruining his life. But by June 1, 1925, Lou played regularly for the Yankees. Altogether, Lou Gehrig played in 2,130 consecutive games in fourteen years, never missing a game. He played in spite of stomach aches, fevers, a sore arm, back pains, and broken fingers. Twice, in 1927 and in 1936, he was voted the American League's most valuable player.

Then, during the 1938 baseball season, Lou stopped hitting. Newspapers reported that he was swinging as hard as he could, but the ball didn't go anywhere. So, he took extra batting practice and tried changing the way he stood. When he hit the ball, however, it still didn't go anywhere. Many other "symptoms" showed up, too; time after time as he swung at the ball, he missed. He even fell down getting dressed and had trouble fielding the ball.

Some people thought Yankee Manager Joe McCarthy should take Lou out of the lineup. But McCarthy refused because of his great respect for Lou. He said, "Gehrig plays as long as he wants to play." Lou told Joe McCarthy on May 2, 1939, "I'm benching myself...for the good of the team."[11]

Very shortly, on June 13, 1939, Lou went to the Mayo Clinic in Rochester, Minnesota for a physical examination. By June 19, Lou's thirty-sixth birthday, the doctors told Lou's wife, Eleanor, that he was suffering from amyotrophic lateral sclerosis, a fatal disease that affects the central nervous system.

Yankee fans and the team celebrated Lou Gehrig's life as a Yankee ball player on July 4, 1939. By that time, he had lost weight and his hair had turned gray, but on that special day, Lou received many honors, even from Mayor Fiorello La Guardia, who commended his sportsmanship and citizenship. When Lou walked slowly to the microphones to address the crowd, all he could tell them was about how "Lucky" he was. By December 1939, Lou Gehrig was voted into the Hall of Fame. He only lived until June 2, 1941, and on June 4, 1941, the day of his funeral, the Yankee game was cancelled because of rain. There were no speeches at his funeral because the minister said everyone present "knew him." Despite his accomplishments as a ball player, Lou Gehrig remained modest and thankful. He always said he was a "lucky man" to have played ball with the New York Yankees.

A Youthful Ailment

Coming into my house from a frigid afternoon of sledding with my favorite sled, "Snow Fiend," I felt a sharp pain in my right ear. I quickly removed my red plaid snow jacket and maroon snow pants and told my mother, "I think I'll lie down for awhile." Now, at eight years of age, "resting" was not a word in my rambunctious life or vocabulary!

The pain in my ear grew worse and was very acute as piercing unseen throbs shot down my entire right side. Finally, my father drove me to the doctor's office where I was diagnosed with an infection of the inner ear. The doctor "lanced" the infection on that first visit, which was nearly as painful as the infection itself. I cried and cried from the pain.

Going to the doctor's office to have my ear treated continued for several weeks, and, of course, I couldn't attend school during this time. But one wonderful day, my Uncle Nelson, a pharmacist from another state, sent some medicine he had discovered that could be applied to my ear. In no time, the pain left and my ear was healed.

Then, I headed back to school amid melting snowdrifts and signs of spring. I was happy to be back in school, but to my dismay, the class had covered several sections of arithmetic during my absence. I caught up quickly with the reading and other subjects, but arithmetic lagged behind, especially since the class learned to tell time while I was gone. Maybe that's why, even today, time seems unimportant. It all goes back to the ear infection I had in the second grade when I was eight, and I became oblivious to time's demands.

"There are nine requisites for contented living: health enough to make work a pleasure; wealth enough to support your needs; strength enough to battle with difficulties and overcome them; grace enough to confess your sins and forsake them; patience enough to toil until some good is accomplished; charity enough to see some good in your neighbor; love enough to move you to be useful and helpful to others; faith enough to make real the things of God; hope enough to remove all anxious fears concerning the future."

Johann Wolfgang Von Goethe (1749-1832)

"Do not be wise in your own eyes;
Fear the Lord and shun evil.
This will bring health to your body
and nourishment to your bones."

Proverbs 3:9, NIV

[10]*Luckiest Man: The Life and Death of Lou Gehrig.* Jonathan Eig. Simon & Schuster. New York, 2005. pp. 19, [10a]20, [10b]21, [10c]23, [10d]25, [10e]26.

[11]*Lou Gehrig: The Luckiest Man,* David A. Adler, Illustrated by Terry Widener. San Diego: Harcourt Brace 1997.

Chapter Ten

Nothing Seems to Work

"Dwelling on Negatives"

"Twixt the optimist and the pessimist the difference is droll: The optimist sees the doughnut But the pessimist sees the hole."

McLandburgh Wilson (fl. 1915)

Thomas Alva Edison, Inventor of the Electric Light Bulb (1847-1931)

"Genius is 1 percent inspiration and 99 percent perspiration" is Thomas Edison's well-known quote that especially applied to his own life. "What seems impossible today, may not be tomorrow."[12]

Thomas Edison, the quintessential American inventor, didn't recognize the word "failure"—it did not exist in his vocabulary. The last of seven children, three of whom died in childbirth, Thomas appeared on February 11, 1847, in Milan, Ohio. His father, Samuel Edison, had a shingle and grain business.

When Thomas was seven, the family moved to Port Huron, Michigan, a thriving port city where his father managed a grocery store and worked in grain and lumber businesses. The bustling town of Port Huron boasted lumber mills, sawmills, shipyards, and foundries, or iron factories. Thomas was fascinated by the machines these factories and industries used.

Most likely, Thomas inherited some of his inventiveness from his father who always looked for extra ways to earn money. An example of his ingenuity was his building a 100-foot-high wooden tower adjacent to the family home. For 25 cents, people could climb the tower and get a spectacular view of the lake and surrounding countryside.

Although Thomas's formal schooling was limited (similar to other children of the time), his mother took over her son's education after he had attended school only for a year and a half. He said of his mother, Nancy Elliott Edison, a former school teacher, "My mother taught me how to read good books quickly and correctly, and as this opened up a great world in literature, I have always been very thankful for this early training."[12a]

An important book that impressed young Edison in his early years was *A School Compendium of Natural and Experimental Philosophy*. Thomas loved reading the book, then went a step further and tried implementing the experiments himself. Some of the topics the book covered were mechanics, acoustics, optics, electricity, magnetism, and astronomy. By doing the experiments, Thomas could learn how things worked. He actually built his own telegraph set from an illustration he saw in the book. He stretched a wire (using batteries attached to it from the kit) from his house to a friend's house half a mile away. They used the dots and dashes of Morse Code over the telegraph.

When he discovered a book on chemistry, he set up a laboratory in the cellar of his house, stocking it with acids and chemicals. He alarmed his parents, however, with occasional explosions. But by the age of 12, Thomas persuaded his parents to let him take a job aboard the Grand Trunk Railway, which had just come to Port

Huron. For the next four years, he sold newspapers, including the *Detroit Free Press*, magazines, candy, peanuts, cigars, and other items to passengers on the daily round trip to Detroit. In addition, he set up a stand selling fruits and vegetables at the Port Huron station.

Often he faced a long layover in Detroit, so the young entrepreneur spent his time in the library reading numerous books on science and technology. Thomas also performed investigations in the baggage car until a chemical spill caught fire one day and put an end to his budding chemistry career.

It wasn't long before the enterprising Thomas set up a printing press in the baggage car, printing his own paper. He was fourteen at the time, and his newspapers contained daily news, which he gleaned from telegraph operators at stations along the way. He included other items of interest like train schedules, birth announcements, gossip, jokes, and market prices for butter, eggs, turkeys, and hogs. A headline in one issue reflected his lifelong attitude toward work: "The more to do, the more is done."[12b]

His hearing began to fail during the years he worked on the train. He remarked at the time that he hadn't heard a bird sing since he was twelve years old. Although he was never totally deaf, Thomas actually considered his hearing loss an asset enabling him to blot out unnecessary sounds and concentrate more on the work at hand.

At the tender age of sixteen, Thomas became a telegrapher, the fastest way to send news at the time. He continued to experiment and soon became a "tramp telegrapher" traveling around the Midwest and south to ply his trade. In the meantime, he studied every aspect of telegraphy but especially the batteries. His experiments enabled him to learn much about how batteries and electricity worked. He preferred to work night jobs, leaving his days free to read and experiment.

When he was twenty-two years old, Thomas got his first patent, an electric vote recorder. But he wasn't satisfied with it because it didn't sell. He had hoped the device would be useful to state legislators, but lawmakers were not interested in buying it. Thomas determined never to invent anything that people didn't want to buy. He said at the time, "Anything that won't sell, I don't want to invent. Its sale is proof of its utility, and utility is success."[12c]

From his early days as a telegrapher, Thomas had the ability to take catnaps—anytime, anywhere. He could stretch out on a couple of chairs and doze off, if necessary. His hearing loss facilitated this ability since he could "tune out" unwanted sounds.

In 1869, Edison moved to New York City and soon started a business called Pope, Edison and Company with a fellow inventor named Franklin Pope. Their company offered a variety of services having to do with devising electrical instruments and solving problems to order. By the time he was twenty-three, the young inventor had earned a reputation as one of the best electrical inventors in the nation, which helped him attract more financial backers. When his partnership with Pope broke up in 1870, Edison opened his very own manufacturing company and laboratory in Newark, New Jersey.

Before long, Edison hired more than fifty employees to make and sell his stock printers and other equipment and to assist with his numerous experiments. Two of the people he hired at that time as skilled machinists and clockmakers were Charles Bachelor and John Kruesi. Each of these men became lifelong friends as well as employees.

By 1871, Edison started his own news service, The News Reporting Telegraph Company. Among the company's employees was a pretty sixteen-year-old clerk named Mary Stilwell, whose father worked in a sawmill. Edison was smitten by the attractive teenager and courted her briefly. The two married on Christmas Day, 1871. Thomas and Mary had three children, two boys and a girl, but Mary always realized she played "second fiddle" to Thomas's work.

Although Edison and his workers, or "muckers" as they were known, came up with many inventions, including the phonograph, talking pictures, and photography, the most well-known and useful one was probably the electric light bulb. Other inventors were trying to come up with this invention, too. By late December 1879, Edison and his "muckers" had perfected the bulb. By 1882, Edison had set up the first electric power station in New York City.

Edison was saddened within two years of his great success by his wife's death at the age of twenty-nine. However, the following year, love visited him again in the person of Mina Miller, a well-educated young woman and the daughter of wealthy parents. After their wedding in 1886, the newlyweds moved to West Orange, New Jersey where Edison had purchased a 29-room mansion called Glenmont for his new bride. Edison, like other men of the era, was not closely involved with his children by Mina: Madeleine, Charles, and Theodore, so they relied on Mina for their upbringing.

After a long and distinguished career, Edison died on October 21, 1931. Complying with a request from President Herbert Hoover, people all over the country dimmed their lights at 10 p.m. for one full minute. All his life Edison lived by the motto: "Negative results are just what I want. They're just as valuable to me as positive results. I can never find the thing that does the job best until I find the ones that won't do."[12d] Edison certainly proved his motto by his challenging life and numerous inventions, many of which we continue to enjoy today.

What's Wrong with Negative Thinking

To begin, negative thinking "saps" your energy and your creativity. Negative thinking also makes a person feel hopeless and like "what's the use" of doing anything. On the other hand, if a person has optimism about his/her life, they will begin to be energized and walk with a spring in their step. They will think "the sky's the limit," and "I can accomplish this," whatever it is. Someone has said, "Shift your emphasis from problems to challenges. Let your mind go to work on finding a solution—a solution is always available—you just need to find it." So don't let problems and negative thinking slow you down and stop you. Hold on, and search for a new outlook that will put you over.

The Mis-matched Corduroys

When my children were three and four years old, I decided to make them matching corduroy trousers. So I dived into my project picking out a cute, print fabric stamped with red, yellow, and green dogs and cats. As I cut out the fabric, I hummed a cheerful tune, thinking how great the finished trousers would be. But when I got the pants cut out, to my dismay, I had cut out the right leg twice with no left leg.

As I thought about what to do, it occurred to me to pick out some new, plain corduroy fabric and have two different colored leg panels. So, I chose some chartreuse corduroy material and sewed the trousers with contrasting leg panels. When my children wore their corduroys out shopping or on errands, people often remarked about how creative and original the trousers were—all because I made a mistake when I cut them out!

"Don't fret or worry. Instead of worrying, pray. Let petitions and praises shape your worries into prayers, Letting God know your concerns. Before you know it, a sense of God's wholeness, everything coming together for good, will come and settle you down."

Philippians 4:6-7 (The Message Bible)

[12]*A Photo Biography of Thomas Edison: Inventing the Future.* Marie Ferguson Delano, National Geographic Society, 2002. PP. Foreword, [12a]9, [12b]12, [12c]21, [12d]51.

CHAPTER ELEVEN

FINDING YOUR STRENGTH AND WILLPOWER

"I Can Get Through This"

"Those who wait upon God get fresh strength.
They spread their wings and soar like eagles.
They run and don't get tired,
They walk and don't lag behind."
(Isaiah 40:31, The Message Bible)

Charles Lindbergh and the Spirit of St. Louis, Epitome of Willpower (1902-1974)

Almost from the time of his birth near Detroit on February 4, 1902, Charles Augustus Lindbergh, Jr. displayed an uncanny self-reliance. Most likely he emulated his grandmother, Louise Caroline, who showed "great bravery" during the Sioux uprising in 1862 near St. Cloud, Minnesota. The Lindberghs fled for their lives to a fort in nearby St. Cloud. While encamped there, she gave birth to a daughter. And, even though Louise Caroline was left with a fear of Indians, sometime later when local Indians stole "a specially designed ax her husband needed, she followed them, demanded the return of the ax, and got it."[13]

75

Charles grew up in Little Falls, Minnesota where many young Swedish immigrants had settled. His parents had a troubled marriage, and when Charles, Sr. decided to run for political office, they knew divorce was out of the question. Charles' mother was a former high school principal with a bachelor's degree in science from Michigan State and a master's degree from Columbia University. Her father and her brother were both doctors. Once Charles' father was elected to office, Charles and his mother spent time each year in Washington, D.C. They stopped in Detroit (where Evangeline Land Lindbergh was from) both on the way to Washington, D.C. and on the return trip.

Charles was a self-sufficient young boy who loved the outdoors. He relished being in Washington only because he was near his father. In Little Falls, however, he fished, swam, and from the age of six, had his own gun, soon becoming an expert marksman. He also wandered through the neighboring woods, collected specimens, and studied woodcraft.

He even tamed a chipmunk, built a raft, and spent untold hours sitting beside the Mississippi. Charles had certain chores to do, which included filling the ice box with chunks of ice. At the age of nine, he devised a unique method of getting the ice from its source into the family icebox.

Although Charles' mother enrolled him in school in Washington, he disliked the classroom setting and never finished a full academic year. The young Lindbergh much preferred an outdoor classroom. At least when he was in Detroit at his mother's parents, he could conduct scientific experiments in his grandfather's laboratory.

One summer when Charles was ten years old, his father drove from Washington with a Model T Ford. The car was for Charles' mother. Charles' legs were too short to reach the car pedals, and he suffered for months watching his mechanically inept parents fail to properly utilize and keep the car in peak running condition.

By the time his father sought re-election in 1913, Charles, Jr., became his chauffeur so his father could campaign all over the district. The campaign was most important to Charles, Sr. He had strong feelings about particular national issues. In fact, unlike many of his constituents, Charles, Sr., was quite liberal in his views; some people thought he was a socialist. In addition, he was critical of the big financiers of the day like the Rockefellers and the Morgans. He even wrote a book called *Banking and Currency and the Money Trust* in which he disdained many common Wall Street practices.

Charles, Sr., also embraced pacificism and opposed U.S. involvement in the Mexican conflict in which President Wilson tried to intervene; neither did he advocate the U.S. involvement in World War I. But like the farmers he represented, he was in favor of the same market protections they advocated and they voted him back to Congress in 1913.

A nice break for Charles, Jr., came in the summer of 1915 when his father was asked by Congress to lead a two-man expedition through the wilderness. The trip's purpose was to seek the source of the Mississippi and draw up a report on its dam system, reported to be in trouble. Charles, Sr., chose his son to be his companion, and for six weeks, the two fought sun, flies, and mosquitos to complete the task. Along the way, they stayed in lumberjack camps and with Indians, who made Charles an honorary member of the Chippewa Tribe. For Charles, Jr., who relished the trip, the time tracing the Mississippi source proved to be a wonderful time for him to get acquainted with his father on a personal level.

In 1916 when seeking the Republican nomination for senator, Charles, Sr., was haunted by two issues from the past: he had been against America's entering World War I, and he had been chosen earlier to investigate charges that the Roman Catholic Church prevented freedom of speech, thought, and conscience. Unfortunately, his heavily Catholic district prevented his senatorial election—and later, his gubernatorial election. His political career was finished with these two defeats.

When the campaign of 1916 concluded, Evangeline and Charles, Jr., drove to California, a trip that took 40 days because of bad weather. They rented a cottage at Redondo Beach and Charles enrolled in the local high school.

However, he was not a good student and preferred to teach himself. He spent his time playing hooky and roamed the beach collecting shells and daydreaming. When Evangeline learned that her mother was seriously ill with cancer and not expected to live. She and Charles, Jr., left at once for Michigan, and for the first time, planned to stay on the farm for the winter. She and her son brought her ailing mother back to Little Falls with them. Charles, Sr., in the meantime, liked the idea of being self sufficient on the farm. The elder Lindbergh turned the entire farm management over to his son, a fifteen-year-old boy.

Charles, Jr., however, relished the opportunity of doing the numerous chores: feeding animals, milking cows, building pigsties, and a duck pond, buying new stock, farm machinery, and repairing the machinery. He slept on a screened-in porch at night, gazing at the sky and the stars.[13a] Fortunately for him, the government decreed that any boy able to work full time on a farm could receive full credit for the period he was out of school. Charles was thrilled. He loved farming, rising at 5:00 a. m. to begin his busy day of chores. He thought farming would be his life; but with the armistice of 1918 and the end of the war, his life completely changed.

After trying a short stint at the University of Wisconsin in 1918 and 1919, Lindbergh realized how much he disliked the structured classroom. For one thing, his fellow students mainly wanted a good time consisting of drinking and smoking, but he abstained from both. Neither did he drink coffee nor cola drinks. He didn't much care for girls, either, thinking them silly. Every night he went home to his mother.

Before long, Charles quit college and went to Nebraska where he enrolled for flight lessons with the Nebraska Aircraft Company. On April 9, 1922, he made his first airplane flight. Later he wrote about the joys of flying: "Aviation combined all the elements I loved.... A pilot was surrounded by beauty of earth and sky. He brushed tree tops with the birds, leapt valleys and rivers, explored the cloud canyon he had gazed at as a child."[13b]

When Lindbergh's instructor turned out to be unreliable, the young man associated himself with a "barnstorming" pilot named Erold Bahl. Bahl was a skilled pilot and Lindbergh wanted to learn everything he could teach him. A "barnstormer" took passengers up in the plane for roughly five dollars a ticket. The two "barnstormed" throughout the Midwest and young Lindbergh learned everything he could about planes and piloting.

Lindbergh was able to buy his own somewhat antiquated plane—a Curtis Jenny—when he borrowed $900 from his father. Both parents flew with their son at different times and were immensely proud of him. But after some time, he sold his plane and joined the army to become an air cadet. This experience completed his knowledge of flying. The difficult course caused many of the students to drop out; in fact, only 18 of the 104 cadets finished the course. Lindbergh graduated at the top of his class and had learned many new techniques: formation flying, high-altitude maneuvers, strafing, bombing, gunnery, photography, and precision take offs and landings. He said about flying that he had "discovered his calling."

Lindbergh flew in a variety of situations after leaving the army. But when he learned of a challenge to fly from New York City to Paris for a prize of $25,000, he decided he would be the pilot to accomplish the feat. Another flyer had attempted the flight, but his plane crashed shortly after takeoff. Other competitors lined up as well.

Lindbergh believed the weight of the plane caused the catastrophe, so he planned for as little weight as possible in his own plane. Ryan Aircraft in San Diego, California, turned out to be the company Lindbergh chose to build his special single engine plane, assisted by some financial backers, including financier Harry Guggenheim. Charles watched over every detail of his specially built plane. And the men who constructed it were equally dedicated. The company put all other projects on hold and "pushed" Lindbergh's plane, *The Spirit of St. Louis* toward a speedy finish.

The day Lindbergh flew his plane for the first time he noted the mechanics and people who had worked on his plane looked on it "as though some child of theirs was going away to war. Their part was done. For them, the flight had started. For two months theirs had been the active part, while I stood by watching their craftsmanship...Now the roles are reversed, and I'll have the field of action. Now, the success of their efforts depends upon my skill; and my life upon their thoroughness."[13c]

The flyer first flew his plane from California (and Ryan Aircraft) all night over the Rockies to St. Louis where he landed on May 11, 1927. His backers planned some elaborate festivities, but Lindbergh was concerned about time and convinced the revelers to hold off. Shortly, he flew on to New York City, his starting point to cross the Atlantic. Then when the weatherman reported clearing weather over the Atlantic, Lindbergh decided once more to forego any pre-planned celebrations and take off at once.

By May 19, Lindbergh and the Spirit of St. Louis were airborne, not without a few minor problems. The flier knew he had enough fuel—in fact, he had 50 hours' worth of fuel, although 36 hours' worth should be sufficient. If he got off course, however, he would need the extra fuel.

He had decided against having a radio because of the extra weight. He relied solely on a compass, a sextant and a chart. He looked only to the Great Arctic Circle Course he had charted himself. As Lindbergh flew over St. John's Newfoundland, he had already flown about eleven hours and it was getting dark. Up ahead, however, loomed the danger of icebergs, and he had to stay alert. Throughout the long, arduous trip, Lindbergh fought sleep and ate little. But every time he drifted off to sleep, the plane began to wobble violently and would wake him up, probably saving his life.

Finally, after flying twenty-seven hours, the aviator saw several small fishing boats and knew the European coast couldn't be far off. Before long, he saw the coast of Ireland—and whole villages of people who waved at him! The word was out that he had made it to Ireland and masses of people looked for him and welcomed him to Europe.

At last, around 10 o'clock at night, Lindbergh spotted the Eiffel Tower, flew around it, then went on to Le Bourget flying field northeast of Paris. A tremendous group of people, roughly 20,000, waited for him and shouted "Lindbergh, Lindbergh, Lindbergh!" A brief time after he landed, Charles Lindbergh was the most famous man in the world. By June 11, 1927 (after numerous celebrations in Europe), Lindbergh headed back to the United States and New York City where between three and four million people celebrated his achievement in a ticker-tape parade on Broadway. Lindbergh died in 1974 from lymphatic cancer after having lived a rather tumultuous and controversial life following his triumphant flight to Paris in 1927. His flight, however, will always be celebrated for the daring feat it was. Initially, he trained and planned the flight with care, monitoring every detail. Throughout history, he will be acclaimed for the great achievement he accomplished.

The Paper Route

"Hey, Sis; how'd you like to earn some extra money? If you deliver the papers on Friday, you can keep all the money," my big brother Ken told me. My two brothers wanted a break from their daily morning paper route of delivering the *Des Moines Register*.

So I was the designated stand-in. At eleven years of age, I felt honored they counted me worthy to take over the route—even for a short time.

I still remember rising in the dark, cold December dawn of northeast Iowa at 5:00 a.m., putting on a couple layers of clothes, including a maroon woolen snowsuit and pulling a red wagon to the paper collection place as the rosy glow of the sunrise had just peeked over the horizon. Around five or six other paperboys had already gathered there; I was the only girl. I loaded up the wagon with papers for 20 or 25 customers.

I finally finished around 7:45 and got back home in time to get ready for school. One day of taking the route was probably enough while my lazy brothers slept in! I don't recall taking the route after that first time, although to hear my brothers say, "You did a great job. We're so proud of you," made it all worthwhile.

Finding Your Will Power

Have you ever had a task too hard to do? Maybe it takes too long or is simply too difficult for your ability. Once you start it, though, you discover that little by little you begin to master the chore. You actually gain in strength and get a "second wind." Runners call this a "Runner's High." It happens when they're fatigued and doubt they can continue; but then the body kicks in and gives them a boost of energy.

Remember, when you don't think you can continue with a difficult task, your own body will come to the rescue with renewed vigor at the right time!

"You gain strength, courage and confidence by every experience in which you really stop to look fear in the face. You are able to say to yourself, 'I lived through this horror. I can take the next thing that comes along'... you must do the thing you cannot do."

Anna Eleanor Roosevelt (1884-1962)
"You Learn by Living," 1960.

[13]*Charles Lindbergh.* Blythe Randolph. Franklin Watts Publishers, New York, 1990, pp. 12, [13a]20, [13b]24, [13c]42.

Chapter Twelve

First Things First

Setting up Guidelines

"But if one should live his life by true principles, man's greatest riches is to live on a little with contented mind; for a little is never lacking."
Lucretius {Titus Lucretius Carus} (99-55 B.C.)

Benjamin Franklin, Guide for American Liberty (1706-1790)

"If you would live with ease do what you ought and not what you please," so noted the young Benjamin Franklin in one of his early pithy sayings.[14]

This bright young boy was the tenth son born to Josiah Franklin, a Boston candle maker, in 1706. Benjamin seemed different from his brothers. He learned to read at the age of four and soon began consuming book after book in his eagerness to learn. Since he lived near the water, he also taught himself to swim and sail.

He was fascinated with the wind as it carried the boats over the water the same way it carried his kite into the sky. One day, he attached the kite to himself as if the kite were a sail and he were a boat. To the amazement of his friends, the kite carried Benjamin over the water just as if he were a sailboat. Because of Ben's many ideas, his friends generally looked to him to lead them.

At eight years of age, Ben's father started him in grammar school where he quickly rose to the head of his class in reading and writing, although he was not that good in arithmetic. His father then thought that Benjamin might do well as a tradesman like his brothers, so his father took him out of school to learn candle-making, his father's trade.

But the young boy was not at all happy dipping candles and cutting wicks all day long. Thus, Benjamin continued to read—and to dream. He thought of far-away ports so much his father feared he would become a sailor and be lost at sea. His father took him to many different business people like joiners, braziers, cutlers, and bricklayers, but Ben didn't care to do any of these jobs. Finally, since he liked words so much, his father decided to apprentice Ben to his older brother, James, in his print shop.

At age 12, Ben moved from his father's house and "bound" himself to James as his apprentice for nine years. Some of his duties included sweeping the floor, washing the type, and doing most of the dirty work of the print shop all the while he watched his brother and others print pamphlets and books. In time, his brother taught him to type and print, in addition to the menial print shop work.

One day he made a bargain with his brother to let him purchase his own food instead of paying him board. After getting his own food, Ben could stay in the shop and read books while the others went out for lunch. Not only did he have time to read, but he saved money by buying his own food and with the extra money, he bought books.

Ben also wanted to be a writer, but he knew if his brother realized it, he would laugh and tell him he was getting too big for his breeches and box his ears. If he became a printer, however, he could publish his own ideas, and if they were interesting and well written, people would read them. To pursue his dreams, young Ben studied the latest London magazines endeavoring to make his own work as good as they were. He copied and cut apart sentences, re-arranged them, then wrote the idea behind each one.

The readers of James Franklin's newspapers received a treat on April 2, 1722, when they read a letter by a Mrs. Silence Dogood. James was happy to receive each subsequent letter and his readers liked them, too. The letters were filled with witticisms about her husband's death, schooling for girls, and fashions. Unfortunately, when James discovered Ben as the author of the epistles, that ended the "Mrs. Silence Dogood" letters.

Ben needed to get away from his bossy older brother. He sold a few of his best books for traveling money, and on a September night he got on board a southbound sloop, as he bid farewell to Boston and his early life. The sloop he was on took him to New York, but he failed to find work there so he traveled on finally ending up in Philadelphia. Ben's luck changed in Philadelphia where he found work with a Mr. Keiner in his print shop.

From there he sailed on to England in 1724 on Christmas Eve. He would try to buy printing equipment for his own shop—the Pennsylvania governor had promised to help him to purchase the equipment. But after two years, the governor failed to keep his word, and Ben was homesick for America. So, once more, in the summer of 1726, he set sail to return home. He conducted some experiments, however, on the voyage. One of them, with a thermometer on a rope, he tested the ocean's temperature and became the first scientist to discover the Gulf Stream. The Stream was a big current of warm water that flowed through the cold sea.

During the journey, he recorded his seaweed experiments and also the sighting of a strange night rainbow arching over the moonlit Atlantic. Ben felt anxious to get on with his life. He entered into his journal new ideas on using his time, his thoughts, and his money. His plans failed to materialize when he returned. His girl friend Deborah had married someone else, the Pennsylvania governor avoided him, and the proposed printing shop partner got sick and died. Then, reverses made him all the more determined to succeed, and he ended up working back at Mr. Keiner's print shop.

In the meantime, Deborah's first husband left the country, and she and Ben revived their old affection. Soon, Ben had a baby son, William, a little boy he adored. Now, Ben's life began to flourish. In his paper, the *Pennsylvania Gazette*, he printed ideas discussed at the "Junto," a young man's club he had started to improve the participants' minds as well as their community. Out of this collaboration of people came a library, volunteer firefighters, paved and lighted streets, and a hospital. These ideas came from Ben's active brain.

Three months after Franklin's son Francis was born in 1732, another brainchild of Franklin's arrived: *Poor Richard's Almanac*. Ben's life overflowed at that time with his family, his club, his printing and writing, and his part-time jobs of Colonial Assembly, Clerk and Town Postmaster.

About the time of his daughter Sally's birth in 1743, Ben had a great idea for his "Franklin Stove," which provided more even heat than any of the day's fireplaces. This invention was followed shortly by his discovery of lightning being composed of electricity. He invented the lightning rod as well to deflect lightning from the roof of buildings. What he discovered was that electricity could be both positive and negative; the question Ben answered in June 1752 with a key and a kite was that lightning and electricity were the same thing. He risked his life doing this experiment, but it brought him worldwide fame and honorary doctor's degrees.

In the following year, by 1776, Ben Franklin served his country by traveling to France to solicit help for the fledgling American army. At first France was unwilling to help, but after the colonists' victory at Saratoga, New York in October 1777, France threw its monetary weight behind the Americans and against the detested British. The French were enthralled by the witty and charming Dr. Franklin. Some of those who came to see him in Paris were Baron Von Steuben, the teenage Marquis de Lafayette—and artists, scientists, Americans needing help, and flirtatious ladies.[15]

Ben's final days in 1787 were perhaps his most illustrious as he worked with the Continental Congress hammering out the differences of opinion in the thirteen colonies. He believed the new government would work as long as the people in it ran it well. He even worked with Thomas Jefferson on the Declaration of Independence doing most of the editing on the document. In addition, he was one of the men who drew up and signed the Constitution of the United States.[15a]

Benjamin Franklin's sparkling wit still showed itself in his Epitaph in 1728 (He died April 17, 1790): "The body of B. Franklin Printer (like the cover of an old book, its contents torn out and stripped of its lettering and gilding) lies here, food for worms. But the work shall not be lost; for it will {as he believed} appear once more, in a new and more elegant edition, revised and corrected by the author."[15b]

Without the wisdom of this remarkable American, our Republic, as we know it, might never have been born. As he noted in his early effort of Mrs. Silence Dogood, July 9, 1722: "Without freedom of thought there can be no such thing as wisdom: and no such thing as liberty without freedom of speech."[15c]

Establishing Priorities

Faced with the final exams for my master's degree in English literature some years ago, I had a decision to make. Was I willing to set aside the majority of extra-curricular pastimes that filled my life like reading *U.S.A. Today,* enjoyable women's magazines like *Woman's Day* and *Redbook,* and attending an occasional movie? Even visiting with friends had to be put on temporary hold. When my friend Julie called asking, "Bonnie, can we meet at this great new restaurant for a salad?" I had to take a rain check.

Studying for these exams for at least six months required every effort I could muster. First, I selected various books for study in my field like a choice book on Herman Melville's *Moby Dick.* Then I planned the hours to study, blocking out for the two classes I was teaching.

I actually looked forward to secluding myself in my cheerful study with its faint, purple-flowered wallpaper and wine-patterned Oriental rug on the polished wood floors. I even bought a pretty teapot with pale red and green flowers on it, and matching cup and saucer. When I entered my study, the teapot (and warmer) waited for me to get busy!

Finally, the time was over and I passed the exams. My life returned to normal. I learned from this experience that anything worthwhile in a person's life sometimes requires a diligent effort, or as wise old Benjamin Franklin said, "Diligence is the mother of good luck." (*The Way to Wealth,* 1758).

"The doors of wisdom are never shut." (*Poor Richard's Almanac,* 1755 Benjamin Franklin)

[14]*Benjamin Franklin*. Ingri & Edgar Parin d'Aulaire. Doubleday & Company. Garden City, New York,1950, p. 4.

[15]*The Remarkable Benjamin Franklin*. Cheryl Harness. National Geographic Society. Washington, D.C., 2005, pp. 43, 35, 43, 29.

CHAPTER THIRTEEN

DETERMINING TO SUCCEED

"It's Too Soon to Give Up"

"Nothing in the world can take the place of persistence. *Talent* will not; Nothing is more common than unsuccessful men with talent. *Genius* will not; Unrewarded genius is almost a Proverb. *Education* will not; The world is full of educated derelicts.

Persistence and *determination* alone are omnipotent. The slogan 'Press On' has solved and always will solve The problems of the human race."

Calvin Coolidge, 30th U.S. President
(1872-1933)

Marie Curie, Discoverer of Radium (1867-1934)

Before leaving for Paris and continuing study, Marie Curie wrote, "Nothing in life is to be feared. It is only to be understood."[16]

Manya Salomee Sklodowski (Marie Curie) already had three sisters and a brother when she was born in Warsaw, Poland, on November 7, 1867. Her father, Wladyslaw Sklodowski, was a mathematics and physics professor while her mother, Bronislawa, directed a private girls school. Poland, at the time, was controlled by Russia, so Manya's early years were somewhat difficult ones.

In fact, Poland was divided among Russia, Austria, and Prussia. Numerous Polish uprisings had taken place against the hated Russian troops, but the Sklodowski family adjusted their lives according to the national situation and they remained staunchly committed to their Polish roots and continued to speak Polish at home. They also adhered to Polish history and culture.

After her father lost his job, Manya's home life changed. Her father began to take in student boarders. The boarders, all young boys, filled the home with lesson recitations, roughhousing and playing tricks on her. Even though studious Manya liked quiet and privacy, she learned to study despite outside disruptions. Because of the boarders, Manya ended up sleeping on a couch in the dining room.

In addition to the boarders bringing in money to the Sklodowski home, they also brought in illness. When Manya was about five, her mother contracted tuberculosis, a bacterial infection of the lungs. Doctors had no medicine at the time to treat the disease and thought the best way to treat the illness was with rest and fresh air. Despite the many precautions of wanting to spare her children from catching any disease, both Bronya and Zosia came down with typhus from one of their boarders. In time, Bronya recovered, but Zosia died from it at age 14. Two years later, Mrs. Sklodowski also died from disease.

Manya attended a private girls' school at this time but for some unknown reason, her father removed her from the school and placed her in a government school. She continued at the school until she was fifteen and graduated first in her class in 1883, winning a gold medal. She wanted to further her education by attending a university as did her sister, Bronya. But they would first have to work and save their money to attend one outside of Poland.

Manya's father realized, however, that she was too sensitive to find work at this time, so he sent her to a relative's country manor in southern Poland. She spent a happy, peaceful year playing tag and shuttlecock, gathering strawberries, and reading books. She also enjoyed conversing with her educated uncles and cousins. Manya wrote to a friend, Kazia: "There are always a great many people, and a freedom, equality and independence such as you can hardly imagine."[16a] She also told her friend about a "Kulig" she attended where there were dancing, festivities, and revelry the entire night until dawn the next day.

On her return to Warsaw, Manya turned sixteen and thought about getting a tutoring or teaching job. Manya continued her education at a "floating university," a forbidden school for girls in Warsaw. She first became interested in science and mathematics at this school. After another year or so passed, Manya had a wonderful letter from her sister, Bronya, who was now studying in Paris and engaged to a young Polish doctor. She urged Manya to plan on coming to Paris to complete her studies within the following year. She would be married by then and Manya could live with her and her husband.

When Manya reached the age of twenty-four the following year, she bid goodbye to her father and siblings and boarded a train bound for France. The 1,000-mile trip took four days from Warsaw to Paris. Manya had no bed and carried her own food, and when she arrived in Paris, she was exhausted. Her new brother-in-law, Casimer Dlaski, met her at the station.

Soon, Manya signed up for classes at the University of Paris (known as the Sorbonne) and registered for classes at the Faculty of Science. She signed her name as Marie, the French equivalent of her Polish-given name, Manya. At this time in 1891, Marie needed to improve her language skills since all the lectures were conducted in French.

She moved from her sister and brother-in-law's apartment to be closer to the university and had to manage on the forty rubles her father sent monthly. The money had to cover rent, food, books, paper, medicine, clothing and any other necessities. Her room had no running water, and her only heat came from a small stove she lit when she could afford a sack of coal. She slept on a folding bed, boiled water on the small stove, and washed her hands and face in cold water. Her diet consisted of tea and bread, and she ate eggs when she had extra money. She quickly became malnourished and went to be with Bronya, who helped her regain her health.

Years later, after she became famous and newspaper reporters called her a sorrowful woman who was willing to isolate herself to carry on her work, Marie noted: "Life is not easy for any of us, but what of that? We must have perseverance and above all confidence in ourselves. We must believe that we are gifted for something and that this thing must be attained."[16] She did not consider it a sacrifice to pursue what she loved: the world of science.

At exam time in 1893, Marie was understandably nervous and had to force herself to focus on the test. But when the results came in several days later, her name was at the top of the list: she graduated with the top honors in her class with a master's degree in physics. She returned for the summer to be with her father in Warsaw but hoped to come back to Paris for further study in mathematics.

Just at the right time, she was recommended for the "Alexandrovitch Scholarship." The scholarship was offered yearly to a deserving Polish student studying abroad. The award amounted to six hundred rubles, enabling Marie to finance fifteen months of study in Paris.

At twenty-six, Marie found another small room in Paris and began work on a second degree. After having had little sleep, she grabbed a cup of tea or chocolate, and possibly some bread from the bakery and walked to the University. Her favorite professor, Gabriel Lippmann, arranged for her to conduct some scientific experiments for which she was paid 600 francs. Her assignment consisted of studying and measuring the magnetic properties of various types of steel.

When her laboratory was too small for the proper implementation of her experiments, a friend recommended a larger laboratory with someone also doing research in magnetism. His name was Pierre Curie. Professor Joseph Kowalski, a Polish professor of physics and a friend of Marie's invited Marie to meet Pierre over tea at his house. Pierre was smitten almost immediately with Marie, but she was reluctant at first to marry, fearing it would deter her plans. In time, however, the two fell in love and married on July 26, 1895, at City Hall. The happy couple left on a bicycling honeymoon when they rode their bikes around the countryside outside of Paris.

Now, Marie needed to return to work. She had finished her research on tempered steels and now searched for a research subject suitable for graduate work—and to complete a doctorate. One thing she lacked, however, was a good laboratory in which to conduct experiments. As he could, Pierre would work with her on the experiments, whatever Marie decided on. The two were finally offered a small, unheated storage space in the school of physics building. Despite the room's dreary aspect, it boasted a black board, wooden tables and a chair, and laboratory equipment.

As Marie looked over scientific journals, she came across a paper written by a physicist named Henri

Becquerel. The French scientist had shown interest in a recent discovery made by a German named Wilhelm Conrad Rontgen, a professor at the University of Wurzburg who had stumbled on the discovery of x-rays by accident. Rontgen was working on cathode rays; these rays are produced when an electric current moves through a vacuum tube. Rontgen and others knew that cathode rays didn't move as light and could be diverted by a magnetic field. No one knew, though, what the rays were and where they came from. Rontgen was only trying to discover if the particles in the cathode rays infiltrated the glass tube. First, he covered a vacuum tube with black paper so he could detect any rays that escaped the tube.

When the scientist first conducted his experiment on November 8, 1895, he noticed that a nearby paper screen coated with a phosphorescent chemical glowed when the current escaped through the vacuum tube and was completely hidden by the black paper. What Rontgen realized is that the rays not only escaped the tube, but they also passed through the paper covering, hitting the screen and leaving an impression.

Rontgen was thrilled with his discovery and continued to do more experiments using photographic plate. The images clearly revealed the bones in his hand. Rontgen called his discovery x-rays—the "x" standing for the mathematical symbol of an unknown quantity.

Many scientists now got involved in studying x-rays, including Henri Becquerel. First, he tried to duplicate Rontgen's experiments but minus the vacuum tube, using phosphorescent materials instead. Initially, he put radium salts, one type of phosphorescent material on photographic paper and put it in the sunlight, which he thought necessary to activate the x-ray. The scientist succeeded in producing an x-ray image of the radium salts with lights, then tried to repeat the experiment using a copper cross.

But the several days of gloomy weather did not cooperate with him, so he wrapped the cross, radium salts, and photographic paper in a black cloth and left everything in a drawer. As the weather cleared, Becquerel pulled open the drawer and to his surprise, a clear image of the cross appeared. Radium salts alone had caused an x-ray image without any light being involved.

Marie determined to continue Becquerel's work since the scientist had now moved on to other projects. Marie subsequently discovered that the atom was not the smallest particle in uranium and that x-rays existed because of something innate in the atom. In March 1898, Marie called the phenomenon radioactivity meaning "ray" from the Latin radius. Another thing she realized was that both uranium and thorium contained radioactivity. She thought that other elements could also contain radioactivity. Pierre helped her with her new search as well.

After hours and hours of painstaking work in the drafty, unheated laboratory working with pitchblende, Marie discovered traces of a radioactive element four hundred times as active as uranium. She called this new element "Polonium" after her homeland. About five months later, Marie discovered another element that registered even higher radiation than polonium. She named the new element "Radium." The Curies worked together with intensity from then on to isolate polonium and radium in their pure states so the scientific community could recognize their achievement. The Curies were awarded a Nobel Prize in Physics on December 10, 1903 (they shared the award with Henri Becquerel at that time).

The Curies continued with other experiments until Pierre's sudden, accidental death in 1906. Marie lived for several more years until she died on July 4, 1934. Although she continued working after Pierre's death and achieved even more honors and recognition, her life was never complete when he no longer worked alongside her. Her exposure to radium undoubtedly undermined her health, and she died in a sanatorium when her bone marrow no longer produced red blood cells. Marie Curie's dedication, long hours of persistence alone are responsible for the discovery of radium, which we enjoy and profit from today.

Running the Peachtree

Training to run the Peachtree Road Race, a 6.2 mile course in Atlanta, Georgia on July 4 was a challenge I'll never forget. Earlier, I hadn't considered running the race, but when I lost twenty some pounds and was already a regular exerciser at the "Y," I thought to myself, "I can do this!"

So, I started jogging laps on the "Y" track, working up after a couple of months to five and six miles. Occasionally, I went outside to jog, but all the jogging I did was on a flat surface—no hills whatsoever. I was so proud of myself as I barely broke into a sweat on my runs.

On race day, I jumped into my red and white jogging gear, and my husband and I drove to Phipps Plaza, the starting point of the race. Lively music played and certain leaders in front led the group in warm-up exercises. Then, we lined up for the race. I was placed in one of the last groups, but I still needed to run a nine-minute mile to get my "Peachtree T shirt." I would show the "naysayers" I could do it!

When the whistle blew starting the race, my adrenaline kicked into overdrive. The first few miles weren't so bad as we ran on fairly flat surfaces, but then we came to "Heartbreak Hill" near Piedmont Hospital in the city. I thought I'd have a heart attack as I pushed with everything I had to conquer the hill, but I hadn't trained on any hilly surfaces!

At last I neared the finish line and crossed it. Near exhaustion, I flopped down on the closest grassy spot—T-shirt in hand—and spotted my dentist, Dr. Kennedy, who had also run the race. Most likely I won't run the Peachtree again but I'm thankful to have run it once. I even wore my Peachtree orange and gray shirt (with a Peach on it!) with a coordinate black jacket and skirt to church the next day as proof that I had conquered the Peachtree Road Race. After the race, we went to eat at Houlihan's where lots of people go to celebrate the Peachtree. Never did barbecue taste so good.

"Success is to be measured not so much by the position that one has reached in life as by the obstacles which he has overcome while trying to succeed."

Booker T. Washington (1856-1915)

[16]*New Elements: The Story of Marie Curie.* Della Yaruzzi. Morgan Reynolds Publishing. Greensboro, North Carolina, 2006, pp 35, 21, 40, 41.

Chapter Fourteen

Asking God's Help and Guidance

"I know God's Listening"

"How do you know," a Bedouin asked, "that there is a God?"

"In the same way," the man replied, "that I know on Looking at the sand, when a man or beast has crossed the desert—by his footprints in the world around me."

Henry Parry Liddon (1829-1890)

Abraham Lincoln, Seeking God's Help at a Difficult Time (1809-1865)

"I claim not to have controlled events but confess plainly that events have controlled me," Lincoln said in the midst of the (American) Civil War that erupted during his first presidential term.[17]

Abe Lincoln, a self-made man, made the most of a difficult situation. Born in a log cabin in Hodgenville, Kentucky on February 12, 1809, Abe's early life consisted of farming, manual labor, and splitting rails. Abe's father, Thomas, grew up as an orphan from the time he was six when Indians killed his father while he worked in the fields. The name "Abraham," Thomas's father's name was long—like the young Abraham Lincoln who stood six feet at the age of twelve.

When Abraham turned seven, the family moved from Kentucky to Indiana where Thomas saw greater opportunity to obtain good land. Here, where the wilderness came nearly to the front door, the Lincolns hewed out lumber from the trees to make a cabin. They carved out more lumber for making tables and benches to use inside.

Some time later, Abraham's mother died following a brief illness. The young boy, his older sister, Sarah, and his father were much saddened by her death. The children's cousin, Dennis, also bereft of Abraham's aunt and uncle who died from drinking "tainted milk" caused by a cow eating poisonous plants, moved in with them. Twelve-year-old Sarah tried to fill her mother's role in cooking and cleaning, but often despaired from weariness.

Over a year later, the family was cheered when Sarah Bush Johnston, a widow with three children, agreed to marry Thomas Lincoln. When Sarah arrived in the Lincoln home, she worked hard and scrubbed the children clean. She even had Thomas cut a hole in the cabin for a window, covering it with greased paper, a substitute for glass at the time. She also had Thomas build an attic room where the three boys could sleep. Sarah loved her new stepson, calling him "The best boy I ever saw or ever expect to see."[18] Abraham even called her "Mama," as she replaced his own mother in his heart.

Sarah Lincoln also encouraged Abraham to attend school, despite the fact that his father thought it unnecessary. Abraham rushed home after school to catch up on chores. Every chance Abe got, though, he read— even in the field at each opportunity. While not many books were available, his stepmother brought a number of them with her from Kentucky. The young boy read the family Bible as well as *The Pilgrim's Progress* and *Aesop's Fables.* His favorite book, though, was *The Life of George Washington.* He liked the book's accounts of the battlefields and the country's struggles for liberty.

His stepmother noted about him, "When he came across a passage that struck him, he would write it down on boards."[18a] When the board was used up, he whittled it down for more use. He practiced over and over and became so good at spelling and writing that illiterate neighbors called on him to compose their letters for them.

Abraham's innate melancholy disposition was tempered by a fun-loving spirit. He even played the part of a ham at times, especially when he mounted a tree stump to imitate local politicians.

At age twenty-one, in the early spring of 1830, Abraham's family moved near Decatur, Illinois to find better farmland. Many settlers moved to Illinois at the same time, clearing the land of its abundant trees and forests. The wood from the trees furnished lumber for homes, fences, and heating. Some of the challenges the Lincoln family faced during their move were: frozen ground just beginning to thaw under a faint spring sun; melting snow flooding the rivers and covering the roads, making the roads muddy and difficult for the oxen to pull their loads; crossing frozen streams, or wading through icy-cold water since there were no bridges. When crossing one frozen river, Abraham's pet dog fell through the ice, so Abraham jumped from the wagon and waded into the waist-high water and pulled his pet to safety.

In the summer and fall, Abraham and his cousin plowed the land (after first building a cabin), and raised a crop of corn. They also built a split-rail fence around ten acres, enclosing the land around the cabin. Unfortunately, the family's troubles worsened in the autumn when they all came down with malaria and fever. During the winter of 1830, deep snow fell for two months and snowdrifts covered the cabin. Then an icy rain fell covering the snowdrifts while temperatures plummeted to zero and stayed there for two months.

Since people stayed in their cabins, cattle froze to death and even wild animals starved to death. With the coming of spring when the snow melted, it flooded the rivers and countryside. In addition, there was little game to hunt. Then cholera struck, killing thousands of people. At last the nightmare subsided. But Abraham felt restless. When a local trader, Dennis Offutt, gave Lincoln and his cousin a chance to take goods on a flat boat to New Orleans, Lincoln jumped at the chance. The trip opened a whole new world to him as he observed slaves being bought and sold and working the fields.

Abraham ended up spending a month in New Orleans before returning home. When he was ready, he booked passage on a steamboat headed for St. Louis; from there, he walked across Illinois to his father's cabin. The man who employed him to take the flatboat to New Orleans now hired him for his general store, plus he could sleep in the back. His employer, Denton Offutt, was very pleased with Abraham, telling everyone how smart and strong he was. Although the average height for a man at this time was five feet six inches, Abraham's height was now six feet four inches.

He was content with his position at the General Store, but not satisfied. Sometime later, Abraham's neighbors asked him to draft deeds and other legal papers for them. Doing these chores plus the local judges asking him to comment on various court cases, led the young man to believe he could run for political office. He lost the election and a short time later, lost his job at the General Store.

Then, he was asked to be the postmaster in New Salem, Illinois. As postmaster, he could read all the papers that arrived in addition to talking with the customers. While still at the post office, Lincoln received the opportunity to be a surveyor. He enlisted the aid of the schoolmaster to help him learn geometry and trigonometry—tools he needed as a surveyor. When he mastered these skills, he set off as a surveyor to plan routes for roads, boundaries and farms. He also met many of the people who later voted for him in the next campaign. He won the next election in 1834 and was elected to the Illinois House of Representatives. He knew he needed to learn the law to do a good job as a state legislator, which he set out to do.

After Lincoln studied for years on his own, he became a lawyer in 1837, and a friend, John Todd Stuart offered him a position in his busy Springfield law office. During that time, too, Lincoln courted Mary Todd, "The Belle of Springfield," and married her in 1842. He also formed a new law partnership with William Herndon, who joined Lincoln's firm as a junior partner. Even though others who saw the Lincoln office called it "a mess," the disorder suited the partners who could usually find what they needed—even in Lincoln's stovepipe hat! Herndon referred to Lincoln's hat as "an extraordinary receptacle, his desk and memorandum book."[18b]

One of his duties every spring and fall was to ride "the circuit" with a judge. The two traveled from one county seat to another holding court and staying at crowded inns. Sometimes as many as twenty men shared a room, some sleeping on quilts spread on the floor. Through these experiences, Lincoln got to know many people who voted him into office at a later date.

Following a series of debates with Stephen Douglas in 1858, Lincoln lost a bid for the Senate. Although he did his best in the debates, he believed he would be forgotten afterward. Instead, the debates with Douglas had brought him national fame and he received numerous invitations to speak. All his speeches paved the way for his presidential election in 1860.

Abraham Lincoln, a self-educated man who suffered many hardships early in his life, always retained a sense of humor. However, he was adamant about slavery and tried to have it outlawed in the District of Columbia after he was elected to the U.S. Senate in 1848 and the Lincoln family moved to Washington, D.C. Lincoln believed slavery was an evil thing in the capital of a country dedicated to liberty.

Lincoln was first elected as President of the United States in 1860 and in January 1863, he signed the "Emancipation Proclamation" announcing the freeing of all slaves then in arms against the United States. Much debate had taken place in the halls of Congress over the issue of slavery, and as each new state came into the Union, a determination had to be made: would it be slave or free?

The U.S. Civil War started in April 1861 and began over the issue of slavery—or "states' rights." The Southern states wanted to retain slavery since almost their entire economy was based on agriculture, and slaves were needed to work the land. Lincoln had his hands full after the war began. He faced various crises including finding good, competent generals and the depletion of the national treasury. The president met each one with a studied coolness and usually came up with the correct response.

By the time of the next presidential election in 1864, Lincoln was voted in unanimously. He still had his hands very full, although the war was winding down. Then on April 9, 1865, General Robert E. Lee, general of the Confederate forces, surrendered at Appomattox Courthouse in Appomattox, Virginia. The terrible war was over. Less than a week later, when Abraham and Mary Lincoln attended a play at Ford's Theater in Washington, a deranged actor, John Wilkes Booth, shot the president and killed him, although Abe lingered for another day or so.

During his tenure as president, Lincoln continually sought guidance from God. He remarked on one occasion, "I have been driven many times to my knees by the overwhelming conviction that I had nowhere else to go." Surely the guidance he received from the Almighty brought the president and the country safely through the War and preserved the Union.

Receiving Help

A few years ago in March, I had finished a necessary project for a college course. I felt gratified but also at a loss as to what to do next, and my finances were low.

That night I got on my knees and prayed, "Lord, if you have work for me to do, please let something come to me. I don't know where to look, Thank You for answering, Amen." With that, I went to bed and slept peacefully.

The next day, about eleven o'clock, the phone rang. The caller was the English Department of a local university. The person on the other end asked, "Would you consider teaching at a nearby school? If you're interested, please call this number."

I called the number as soon as possible. The woman I spoke with asked, "Could you start today? You're an answer to prayer!" Of course the phone call was also an answer to my prayer.

The following day, I started teaching three Research Paper classes, which continued until school was out in June. That night I gave profuse thanks to God for answering prayer and providing me with a good job.

---

[17]*Abraham Lincoln, The Writer: A Treasury of His Greatest Speeches and Letters.* Compiled and Edited by Harold Holzer. Boyd Mills Press, Honesdale, PA, 2000, p.47.

[18]*Abraham Lincoln.* Janis Herbert. Chicago Review Press, Inc., 2007, pp. 8, 8, [18a]16, [18b]39.

CHAPTER FIFTEEN

ACCEPTING HELP FROM OTHERS

"There's no shame in asking for help"

"Ask, and it shall be given you; seek and you shall find; knock. and it shall be opened unto you: For everyone that asks receives; and he that seeks finds; and to him that knocks, it shall be opened."

(Matthew 7:7-8, KJV)

Booker T. Washington, Leader and Educator (1856-1915)

Controversial almost from the beginning of his distinguished career, Booker Taliaferro Washington was born into slavery on a tobacco farm in Franklin County, Virginia on April 5, 1856 (approx.). His mother, Jane, was the plantation cook, and his father was an unknown white man. Booker confessed that his "life had its beginning in the midst of the most miserable, desolate, and discouraging surroundings."[19] He knew little of his ancestry since slave records were not usually kept at that time. His father was a white man from a nearby plantation, but Booker never knew anything more about him. He never found any particular fault with him, however, seeing him as another victim of the "peculiar" institution of slavery.

111

Booker's living quarters (the cabin) also served as the Plantation kitchen. He and his two siblings, his brother, John, and sister, Amanda, slept side by side on a pallet of rags on the cabin's dirt floor.

One of Booker's early jobs at the Plantation was to haul corn to be ground to the mill. Someone would place the heavy bag on the back of the horse and the young boy would lead him to the mill. But often, the bag would fall off the horse, then Booker had to wait until a passer-by arrived to help him.

As far as family meal times, Booker recalls only that the children usually "picked up in whatever fashion they could: a piece of bread here, a scrap of meat there. They never sat down to eat a meal together as a family. Sometimes, too, "a portion of our family would eat from the skillet or pot, while someone else would eat from a tin plate, held on the knees."[19a]

When he grew a little older, Booker was summoned to the "big house" at meal times to fan flies from the table by means of paper fans that operated by a pulley. While he operated the pulley, the young boy absorbed the dinner table conversation, which revolved around freeing the slaves and the war. Even if one of the white masters was killed in the war, the slaves often felt grief and sadness, too.

The day the war ended, great rejoicing broke out at the Plantation. The news had been prepared for by the slaves for sometime as they gleaned information from the "grapevine telegraph." All the slaves were summoned to the "big house" to hear the important news: they were free, could go where they wanted to go, and do what they wanted to do. A stranger read a document to them (probably the Emancipation Proclamation) declaring their freedom. Intense gloom followed the rejoicing as the freed people began to wonder what to do.

The seventy or eighty-year-old slaves had already lived their most productive years. What could they do now? Some of the slaves elected to stay with their "old mar'sters" and "old missus" and arranged to do so. Many of the former slaves also determined to leave the plantation (at least for a few days) to know that they were really free, and second, they now must change their names. In Booker's case, his family moved to a place in West Virginia to join his stepfather, Washington Ferguson.

When Booker lived in West Virginia, the freed slaves had agreed to open a school and Booker looked forward to it eagerly. He worked at the time in a salt furnace and his stepfather realized that he brought in considerable money in his work, so he refused to let him go to school. The young boy was bitterly disappointed but did not give up on his dream.

Then Booker's mother stepped in, suggesting maybe he could work with the teacher in the evenings, which he did. Later on he was able to attend "day school," too, by working so many hours at the salt furnace before and after his classes. Booker also gave himself a name at the school: he had always been known as "Booker," so he kept that, but his mother said she had named him "Booker Taliaferro" when he was born, so he added that to the "Booker Washington," becoming Booker Taliaferro Washington.

One day while he was at work in the salt mine, Booker heard two men talking about a "great school for colored people" somewhere in Virginia. Then and there, he determined to go to the school. His plans to attend Hampton gained momentum when he found another job opportunity with a Mrs. Violet Ruffner. He did house cleaning for her, and although at first he feared being able to please her, he tried as hard as he could to do just that. After some time, Booker and Mrs.

Ruffner "understood" each other, and he worked for her longer than anyone else—about a year and a half.

After that time, with few funds available, Booker set off for Hampton Institute 500 miles away. He walked, begged rides in wagons and somehow finally reached Hampton, but he was hungry, tired and dirty from his journey. Presenting himself to the head teacher for direction, he could see the disdain in her face for the way he appeared. After some time passed, the head teacher told the young man, "The adjoining recitation room needs sweeping. Take a broom and sweep it."[19b] Booker got to work sweeping the recitation room three times, dusting the woodwork around the walls, benches, tables, and desks three or four times. Then he reported back to the head teacher. She inspected his work and was very impressed. Afterward, she deemed him able to enter the institution. To Booker, his entrance into Hampton was a dream come true.

After graduating from Hampton in June 1875, Booker went back to his home in Malden, Virginia, where he began teaching at the school for freed slaves and their children. He even included brushing teeth, washing hands and faces, and other hygiene good habits in the lesson schedule.

Sometime later, after Booker had returned to Hampton to do some teaching, he received an opportunity to go to Tuskegee (Alabama) to head up the Normal School for "Colored" students there. Booker was willing to try, although it was a tall order. Arriving at Tuskegee, the young teacher discovered a scarcity of buildings, teaching materials, but not students. So Booker had to locate suitable buildings first of all, and next, obtain books and other teaching materials. In time, Booker was able to receive many donations and build up the school. The Tuskegee students themselves built many of the buildings as well as doing other work on the buildings.

Booker was quickly put in the position of raising money for the Institute. He traveled throughout the South giving speeches and raising funds for Tuskegee. Fortunately, in his days at Hampton, he had received some training in public speaking. When he was invited to speak at the Atlanta Cotton States and International Exposition in Atlanta on September 18, 1895, he caused an uproar.

As he responded to the race question in his address, Booker advocated a "separate but equal" policy. He said, "In the future, in our humble way, we shall stand by you with a devotion that no foreigner can approach, ready to lay down our lives, if need be, in defense of yours....In all things that are purely social we can be as separate as the fingers, yet one as the hand in all things essential to mutual progress."[19c]

In spite of his being an outstanding teacher, writer and speaker on Black problems in the 19th century, his views were widely applauded at the time. Sometime later, other Black leaders like W.E.B. Du Bois strongly criticized him. And in the 20th century, Civil Rights leaders took much exception to Booker's ideas. Nevertheless, Booker Washington did much to assist the Black race following the Civil War. He also greatly promoted black education through his efforts as a leader, teacher, and speaker at Tuskegee Institute, largely because he was not afraid to solicit help for the school wherever he could find it.

Booker lived an amazing life and pulled himself up by his bootstraps and endured much deprivation in his desire to get an education. His life was exemplary despite the criticism leveled against him after the Atlanta Cotton States Address in 1895. His dream was to better his own race and build up Tuskegee Institute, which to a great extent he accomplished.

Lending a Helping Hand

Following a big snowstorm when we lived in Connecticut, my husband saw our French-Canadian neighbor frantically shoveling his driveway. He opened the door and called out to him, "Lucien, do you need some help?" We lived in a semi-rural area and snowplows probably wouldn't come for some time.

When our neighbor said he'd like help, my husband grabbed his black plaid wool jacket and red snow shovel and hurried out to clear the driveway. The two men shoveled close to an hour until the drive was clear. Then Lucien and his wife got into their Chevrolet and drove to the hospital where she underwent surgery.

We found out later that they had an emergency situation and needed to get to the hospital quickly. Our relationship with our neighbors was much improved after my husband helped shovel their driveway, and we became good friends. Earlier we'd had a cordial, but distant relationship. I think the golden rule applied to this situation: "Do unto others as you would have them do unto you."

"Humility is a virtue all preach, none practice; and yet everybody is content to hear."

John Seldon (1584-1654)

[19]*Up from Slavery,* Booker T. Washington. Random House, New York, 1999. p. 3; [19b]p.8, [19c] p. 35; [19d]pp. 144, 145

CHAPTER SIXTEEN

NOT LETTING LIFE'S DISAPPOINTMENTS TAKE OVER

"This Won't Defeat Me"

> "'Blessed is the man who expects nothing, for he shall never be disappointed was the ninth beatitude.'"
> Pierre Carlit de Chamblain (1688-1763)
> (Letter to Fortescue—September 23, 1728)

Amelia Earhart, The Unstoppable "Lady Lindy" (1897-1937)

Amelia Earhart rarely knew the word "defeat." From the beginning of her flying career, she shared a determination and resolve that enabled her to be the first woman to fly across the Atlantic.

Who was this unusual woman? Amelia Earhart made her first appearance in Atchison, Kansas at the home of her maternal grandparents, Alfred and Amelia Otis, on July 24, 1897. Her grandfather, Judge Otis, was a descendant of American Revolutionary statesman, James Otis. The Judge had traveled from New York state in 1854 to make his new home in Atchison. A few years later, in 1862, he returned to Philadelphia and married Amelia Harris who lived in the city.

117

After building a substantial brick house high on a bluff overlooking the Missouri River, the Otis Family set about raising a large family of eight children. Amelia's mother was the fourth child, Amy. Amy was a good dancer and a fine horsewoman and popular with the young Atchison Society. Amy was also intelligent and cultured, preferring to spend her evenings talking politics with her father's friends. She decided against college following a long illness; instead, she traveled with her father on his western business trips and even climbed Pike's Peak in 1890—the first woman to do so.

Amy's parents wanted her to marry well but she fell in love with a young, good-looking attorney, Edwin Earhart, an impoverished law student. At Amy's coming-out ball in 1890, Amy and Edwin danced the night away as if they only had eyes for each other. They were soon engaged, but Amy's father, tough Judge Otis, forbad them to marry until Edwin could earn at least $50 a month. After his graduation from law school, Edwin got a job selling insurance for a Midwestern railroad. He earned the required $50 per month and Judge Otis gave Amy permission to marry Edwin.

The young husband was often gone for long periods of time, so Amy moved back to her parents' home in Atchison. Her first child had been stillborn, but the second, Amelia Mary, arrived as a healthy newborn. Not long after, the Earharts had a second daughter, Muriel.

Amelia and Muriel roamed the spacious grounds surrounding the Otis home. They searched for arrowheads and played pioneers and Indians. Amelia's active mind always sought new adventures. One of her early projects "was a makeshift roller coaster... Working with the quiet determination that was to become her hallmark, Amelia used fence rails to build tracks leading down the steep slope of a shed roof to the ground."[20] Amelia then made a cart from a plank with old roller skate wheels. All went well as Amelia modified her roller coaster by extending the tracks and made it work much better. Her grandparents, however, deemed the invention "unsuitable" for young girls and took it apart.

Grandmother Otis told the girls the most daring thing she ever did as a young girl was to roll her hoop around the public square. But Edwin and Amy were permissive parents, allowing their daughters to wear unconventional "trousers" and do unladylike things like playing baseball and going fishing.

In the winter when most girls in Atchison sat primly upright on their sleds with wooden runners, Edwin bought his daughters boys' sleds with steel runners. One day, while she lay on her stomach on her sled, Amelia shot down the hill. She glanced up to see a horse and buggy right in her path. She shouted to the driver, but he couldn't hear her, so she "swiftly chose a course of action and followed through on it. Aiming her sled between the front and hind legs of the horse, she closed her eyes and shot down the hill. She streaked safely under the horse—no doubt leaving the driver to wonder what young ladies were coming to these days."[20a]

When Edwin Earhart received a job promotion with the railroad in Des Moines, Iowa in 1905, the family rejoined him. There, at the Iowa State Fair, Amelia saw her first airplane. "'It was a thing of rusty wire and wood and looked not at all interesting,' Amelia noted later."[20b] The airplane's first appearance in her life did not interest her in the least.

With the family move, a change came over Edwin Earhart. He began drinking with his hard-drinking co-workers. They were men who showed him warmth and respect, something he never received from the Otises. When Amy's mother died in 1911, Edwin realized that she had stipulated in her will that Amy's portion of the family fortune be put in trust for twenty years—or until her son-in-law's death; he was devastated. After being fired by the railroad, Edwin's alcoholism increased, causing the family to move often. Because of the family's many moves, the girls attended numerous schools. Amelia finally graduated from high school in 1915 in St. Paul, Minnesota, although she did not receive her diploma at that time. In fact, the mayor of Chicago presented the diploma to her in 1932 at a civic reception several years later.

The family then rejoined Edwin who had set up a law practice in Kansas City. He contested Mrs. Otis' will and achieved a settlement of $60,000, enough to send both girls to college. Muriel chose St. Margaret's in Toronto, Canada, and Amelia enrolled in the Ogontz School, a two-year "female" college near Philadelphia. Her college days were filled with lectures, opera visits, tennis, horseback riding and art classes. The head mistress at Ogontz, Abby Sutherland, said of Amelia, "She was always pushing into unknown seas in her reading. The look in her straight forward eager eyes was most fascinating in those days. At that period her purse, as well as her innate tastes, required the fewest and simplest clothes. But she helped very much to impress the overindulged girls with the beauty and comfort of simple dressing."[20c]

Going to Toronto to visit Muriel in 1917, Amelia was much taken by the wounded veterans she witnessed. She couldn't return to sequestered Ogontz; instead, she began work at a veteran's hospital doing whatever she could. The war ended in November 1918, but Amelia had already come down with a severe case of sinusitis. She and her mother went to visit Muriel, who now attended Smith College in Northampton, Massachusetts while Amelia recovered. While in Massachusetts, Amelia signed up for a class at Smith on automobile engine repair. Later, moving with her mother to New York City, Amelia attended Columbia University where she took an "overload" of classes in order to pursue a medical career. But when Amy and Edwin reunited in Los Angeles and invited Amelia to live with them and finish her studies there, she obediently left for L.A.

Although Amelia met an attractive man, Sam Chapman, in California, her attention was more drawn to aviation. She wanted to take flying lessons in California after attending a number of air shows. The lessons were expensive—around $1000 to teach a student to fly. Amelia, however, found a job to supplement the cost of the lessons: she was smitten with the flying bug. Her flight instructor, Nita Snook, had graduated from the well-known Curtiss School of Aviation.

Snook insisted that Amelia learn the name and function of every part of the training plane before the first take off. The novice pilot first trained in a Curtiss biplane that had dual controls for both Amelia and Nita Snook. At first Earhart practiced take offs and landings, then when her instructor was satisfied with the basics, Snook taught her various aerial maneuvers and other stunt-flying techniques. A student must be thoroughly familiar with every phase of "stunting" so they are prepared to cope with any possible emergency that arises in flight. Earhart notes in her book *Last Flight:* "The fundamental stunts are slips, stalls, loops, barrels, and rolls....Unless a pilot has actually recovered from a stall, has actually put his plane into a spin and brought it out, he cannot know accurately what these acts entail."[20d]

Amelia loved talking shop with the veteran pilots at the airfield, many of whom had flown in World War I. From the beginning of her flying lessons, she wanted her own plane. She bought it on her twenty-fifth birthday: a second-hand bright-yellow Kinner Canary. In exchange for free hangar space, she found employment with W.G. Kinner. Amelia demonstrated the Kinner plane to prosperous buyers, and by the summer of

1922, she received her pilot's license. In the meantime, she gave up her plans to return to college and even to marry the young man, Sam Chapman. However, she was not ready to settle down just yet, or maybe never. She told Sam that she had no wish to become a "domestic robot."[20e]

After her first solo flight, Amelia saved her money for advanced flying lessons. Before long, Earhart began to set records, the first when she flew to 14,000 feet in October 1922. Following her parents' divorce in 1924, the three Earhart women moved East where Amelia found work as a Boston social worker. She had reluctantly sold her plane and bought a car nicknamed the "Yellow Peril." The patients at Denison House were fond of Amelia, and she took a personal liking to each of them. And, although Amelia liked her new job and thrived on it, she could never quite forget the thrill she had flying her yellow Canary over the mountaintops.

At a new crossroads, Amelia received a call that would change her life. The call came from a Captain Hilton Bailey. "You're interested in flying, I understand... would you be willing to do something important for the cause of aviation?" Amelia came back, "Such as what?" "Flying a plane across the Atlantic Ocean."[20f]

Of course, Earhart replied, "Yes," with her customary cool detachment. The flight was a friendship gesture between England and the United States. By mid-May 1928, the plane "Friendship" was ready for takeoff. After a series of delays, however, the plane finally roared into the sky (in Newfoundland) on June 17, 1928. The flight was a success as the plane reached Burry Port, Wales, twenty some hours later. The "Friendship" flight's success (though Earhart didn't pilot the plane) thrust Amelia into a whirlwind of activities: speaking, writing, books, lecturing, and even getting married to G.P. Putnam, a prominent New York publisher. She also taught a course on aviation at Purdue University.

American women loved her short, tousled hairstyle and many emulated it. Amelia also kept flying whenever she could and preparing herself for future flying ventures.

Roughly four years later, Amelia flew solo over the Atlantic, landing on Londonderry Island. Earhart said of her flight: "To want in one's heart to do a thing for its own sake, to concentrate all one's energies upon it—that is not only the surest guarantee of its success, it is also being true to oneself."[20g] Once more, Amelia was thrust into a round of parties and celebrations in her honor. She received more accolades in Paris, Rome, and finally, in Washington, D.C., where President Hoover presented her with the National Geographic's prized Special Gold Medal for distinction in aviation. After the adulation had died down, however, Earhart looked for new goals to achieve.

The planned around the world flight of Amelia Earhart in the summer of 1937 came to a screeching halt with her disappearance after the last radio transmission at 8:45 a.m. on July 3, 1937. A gigantic search got under way for Earhart and her plane but to no avail. People set forth many theories as to what had happened to her such as the plane went down in the Pacific or the Japanese had captured her and killed her. However, none of these theories were ever proven.

Some of the qualities that set Amelia Earhart apart in her day—and in our own—are her integrity, courage and determination. These qualities and lesser ones enabled her to succeed as a woman when she faced countless odds because of her refusal to accept defeat when it seemed all hope was gone.

Adventure in Spelunking

Have you ever visited a cave? A number of limestone caves existed in the area where I grew up, and you could pay to go into some of them. But these caves were well lighted and seemingly involved little danger of one's getting lost in them.

My son challenged his dad and me on one occasion to go "spelunking" or caving with him near Stone Mountain, Georgia. Not wanting to disappoint him, I said, "Sure, Steven, we'll go with you"—but I half meant it!

After changing into "old grubby" clothes and sneakers, we were ready. When we got to the cave site, Steven went down the steep, dark steps first, followed by me and then his dad. The only light we had was a little lantern. Needless to say, we clung to each other inside the cave so we wouldn't get lost. What struck me in the cave was the complete and utter blackness of the cave interior. It was impossible to see anything without the aid of a lantern or light of some kind. I suppose we stayed in the cave almost twenty minutes, although it seemed like an eternity. We climbed back out before panic set in! My son didn't panic, but his parents almost did.

Next time you visit a cave, think of what the cave would be like without any light. I'm thankful today that I don't have to live in a cave and that I have all the light I need with the flick of a switch.

[20]*Amelia Earhart: Aviator*. Nancy Shore. Chelsea House Publishers, NY, 1989. pp. 23, [20a]24-25, [20b]25, [20c]29, [20d]30, [20e]37, [20f]45, [20g]71

CHAPTER SEVENTEEN

RETHINKING SOLUTIONS

"If at first I don't succeed, try again"

> "'Tis better to have tried in vain,
> sincerely striving for a goal,
> than to have lived upon the plain
> an idle and a timid soul.
> Tis better to have fought and spent
> your courage, missing all applause,
> than to have lived in smug content
> and never ventured for a cause.
> For he who tries and fails may be
> the founder of a better day;
> though never his the victory.
> From him shall others learn the way."
>
> Edgar Guest (1881-1959)

Dale Carnegie, Success or Failure? (1888-1955)

Dale Carnegie, author of the well-known book, How to Win Friends and Influence People, struggled early on to be a success in life. Carnegie became famous for his book, yet in his own speaking he seemed rambling and incoherent, and his Midwestern twang added little to his delivery. Even when his book was the number one best-seller, he experienced astonishment at his fame. In the course of his career, Dale found himself branded as "cynical, conniving, and manipula-tive."[21]

Who was this paradoxical person? Born on No-vember 24,1888, Dale Carnegie grew up on a small, impoverished farm in Northwest Missouri near the "102" River. Yearly, the river flooded the fertile farm-land at harvest time, wiping out what might have been a bountiful harvest of corn and drenched the hay. In ad-dition, "Season after season, the fat hogs sickened and died from cholera, the bottom fell out of the market for cattle and mules, and the bank threatened to foreclose the mortgage."[22]

Dale's early family life revolved around the farm, home, and Harmony Methodist Church. The family moved numerous times in Dale's early years, finally settling on a farm in 1904 near Warrensburg, Missouri, about fifty miles south of Kansas City, Missouri. The family made their final move so Dale could attend War-rensburg State Teachers College and not have to board. Students preparing to teach could attend tuition free so that's what Dale did, riding his horse back and forth over the three miles each day.

Conscious of his tattered, patched clothing in col-lege, Dale struggled to excel at something. He was a mediocre student, not because he lacked the drive to excel but because of the hardness of his life. His father told him about a difficult time in his own life when the family still lived on the Maryville farm in 1898. Dale's father had been turned down for a loan request by a Maryville banker who had threatened to foreclose on the farm. On the way home he crossed the bridge over the 102 River. The accumulation of debts, the incessant toil, discouragement, and worry fastened on him in an unrelenting grip. He stopped the buggy, gazed at the tumultuous current, contemplated leaping in and end-ing it all. Dale's father told him later, "If it had not been for mother's religious faith, he would not have had the courage to live through those terrible years."[22a]

Another chore Dale remembered doing when he was growing up was taking care of newborn piglets. He says of that responsibility (usually in February): "The last thing I did before I went to bed at night was to take that basket of pigs from behind the kitchen stove out to the hog shed, wait for them to nurse, and then bring them back and put them behind the stove."[22b] The whole process was repeated a few hours later after which he got up to study his Latin verbs.

In college, Dale had had some success in speaking and debating. He realized he could win approval by applying these skills, so that's what he tried to do after leaving college. He tried sales and a few other jobs, and though he did well, the jobs had drawbacks, too. Finally, Dale headed to New York seeking to fulfill a desire to get into show business.

When he reached New York City, miraculously the American Academy of Dramatic Arts accepted Dale as a student. The Academy emphasized being natural and sincere as actors. Edward G. Robinson was a fellow student with Carnegie and left the school to succeed in Hollywood later on. The Academy's director, Charles Jehlinger, had issued the following statement regarding the school's principles (two years before Carnegie entered the school): "To create an accent on naturalism accompanied by emotional recall in order to achieve a deeper, more essential 'truth' in performance."[22c] This statement of purpose is close to what Carnegie would teach in public speaking later in his own courses.

After a brief acting debut with a travelling actor's group, Dale needed to find a way to earn a living. So he approached the program director of the 125th Street YMCA in New York City. The "Y" already advertised a "Harlem Evening School" and Dale thought he could teach Public Speaking in an evening class. The director said he could present his ideas at a social evening. When Dale's turn came, he recited a poem by James Whitcomb Riley called "Knee Deep in June." The recitation met with applause and Dale was hired to teach a night session of public speaking at $2 per session.

The first session, however, was nearly the last. Dale looked at a sea of blank faces and knew he was in trouble. The tutoring techniques he practiced in college weren't working with these businessmen. He called on a man in the back row to talk about himself. Before long, the class "took off." The key was getting class members on their feet talking about topics they knew, usually about themselves. Three seasons later, Dale earned $30 a night in commissions.

The course continued to grow and evolve as Dale improvised on the classes. With the publication of his book, *How to Win Friends and Influence People* in 1936, Dale's income was assured. Because of the book, people now came to Carnegie wondering where they could take the course. Many well-known people signed up for Carnegie's courses, including Lee Iacocca and Lowell Thomas, who became a life-long friend. Today, the book has gone through hundreds of editions and countless revisions and updates. Lowell Thomas endorsed the Carnegie Course, calling it "Unique," a combination of public speaking, human relations and applied psychology."[22d] At last, Dale Carnegie had achieved a greater success than he ever dreamed—far away from the 102 River and Warrensburg State Teachers College in Missouri—all because he used the skills he already had and built an amazing course from them. He enabled millions of people all over the world to become more effective in their lives than they ever dreamed possible.

When I Almost Failed Swimming at Eighteen

Swimming was my life when I enrolled in a small midwestern college. Every quarter, I made sure I could fit a swimming class in, learning the Australian crawl (free stroke), back stroke, and side stroke, among other courses. I braided my long, dark brown hair and pulled the braids across the top of my head. It stayed wet most of the time! I had an excellent teacher, too, and had a great relationship with her. Since my coordination was good, Ms. Winsberg used me to demonstrate correct strokes in the pool.

I began to take my favored position for granted, but at the beginning of one quarter, Louie, my boss at the drugstore where I worked, asked me to work earlier than usual. He said, "Bonnie, can you come to work tomorrow morning at 10:00 instead of in the afternoon? I'm expecting a busy day and could use your help." So I said, "Sure, I'll come in at 10:00," even though my first swimming class started at 10:00.

Things went smoothly until I reappeared at my next swimming class. Ms. Winsberg was decidedly irritated with me because I missed the first class. All quarter she dangled me, threatening to fail me in swimming!

I came out of the class with a "C," but I learned an invaluable lesson: Don't presume on people or take them for granted. If I had talked to Ms. Winsberg about my job and told her I was needed at the drugstore, she probably would have understood. I learned one of my great "Life Lessons" through this experience.

Learning from Dale Carnegie

Whatever your situation, it's always too soon to quit. Examine all aspects of your dilemma and ask yourself: Is there another way to solve my problem? Dale Carnegie started teaching Public Speaking at the "Y" and his course over time became an international success in a way he never dreamed possible.

Who knows, but what you may be able to do the same thing.

Tribulation

"God help me to remember that life is full of tribulation. And though You do not always deem it right or wise to help me, yet you are helping me simply by being there.

My strength comes from You. Thank You.

My courage comes from You. Thank You.

Deep, deep within me, implanted by your very hands, is my determination, my toughness, my will to survive."

Marjorie Holmes
"I've Got to Talk to Somebody, God"

[21]*Dale Carnegie: The Man Who Influenced Millions.* Giles Kemp and Edward Claflin. St. Martin's Press, New York, 1989, p. 2.

[22]*How to Win Friends and Influence People.* Dale Carnegie, Simon & Schuster, New York, N.Y., 2009, pp.243, [22a]17, [22b]21, [22c]45, [22d]159.

CHAPTER EIGHTEEN

EATING WISELY

"Little Miss Muffet
Sat on a Tuffet,
Eating some curds and whey,
Along came a spider,
And sat down beside her,
And frightened Miss Muffet away."

Anonymous Nursery Rhyme

Dr. Robert Atkins, author: *Dr. Atkins' New Diet Revolution (1930-2003)*

"The best way to describe Dr. Robert Atkins is that he was a pit bull of a man. He chanced upon his controversial ideas about carbohydrates and diet in the early 1960's and hung on unyielding to critics, until the day he died, forty years later."[23]

Interestingly, author Lisa Rojak classified Dr. Atkins as both outspoken and shy, generous and defensive... and he loved working with his patients."[23a]

Where did this controversial person come from? Robert Coleman Atkins was born October 17, 1930, to Eugene and Norma Atkins, descendants of Russian Jews, in Columbus, Ohio. Their marriage was not an arranged one because her father didn't want Norma to marry Eugene. Norma, however, was anxious to leave home. The groom listed his occupation as "Confectioner," a commodity that his son would spend much of his life railing against.

As a young boy, Robert often went with his father on his sales rounds; Eugene even let his young son close a sale or two. The customers sometimes called the little boy "a chip off the old block," but Robert learned valuable lessons even then about dealing with people.

The family moved to Dayton, Ohio, in 1941 where Eugene opened the "Four Aces Bar" at 1115 West 3rd Street, a major city thoroughfare. Norma didn't like the long hours her husband spent at the bar, but he reminded her that if business continued to improve, they could move to a better home in another part of the city. Robert enrolled in the seventh grade at the new location. He worked hard at his studies and was a model student. Some of the lessons Robert's mother taught him at this time concerned the importance of dressing well and also to appreciate fine art. He took the things his mother told him to heart and tried hard to please her.

By his senior year, Robert had achieved scholastic excellence at Fairview High School. The school selected him as one of two students to take a general scholarship test sponsored by the state of Ohio. In preparation for the exam, he studied with another selected student, Robert Rafner. Rafner noted that "Bob was very ambitious intellectually, much more than I was... .I was envious because he played basketball, worked on the school newspaper, went out with any girl who came along, and breezed right through school with top grades, while I had to work so hard at it."[23b] When the scholarship results came in, Robert Atkins had placed second out of 8,500 students from 1,300 high schools in the state; his photo made the cover of the Dayton Herald.

After high school, Robert chose to attend the University of Michigan planning to study medicine. Once more, he chose academic excellence, and before long, he achieved top grades in every class he took. He also pledged to a Jewish Fraternity, Zeta Beta Tau, in addition to developing a flair for comedy routines. While at the university, he made Phi Beta Kappa and was known as a ladies' man dating many different women.

Finishing college, Robert Atkins chose to attend Cornell Medical School in New York City. After a brief adjustment time, he settled in to study and get through the toughest course yet. Then, when he graduated from med school on June 8, 1955, he had to decide where to spend his residency. Atkins chose Rochester University instead of one of the nearby New York City hospitals where most of his classmates went.

After a year at Rochester, however, Atkins came back to New York City to finish his residency—probably after some kind of ruckus he caused with the mostly Gentile medical staff. Even then, Robert had little use for traditional medicine. He always looked for alternate ways to accomplish healing and to promote better health.

Following his residency, Robert chose to be a "freelance" cardiologist rather than be tied to a traditional hospital. By doing so, he was able to build up his practice and not have to answer to anyone else. A colleague from the early 1990's, Bernard Rapler, M.D., said of Atkins, "He was a maverick early on, and not just in terms of weight loss. I think he always had his own ideas about the best way to do things, and I think he never quite trusted what he was taught in medical school."[23d] In addition, Robert wanted to be in a position to urge people to re-examine their own ideas.

When he was setting up his medical practice, Robert sought out business "corporate" stars. Then, because he often worked on call in the emergency room at night, many of his emergencies came from New York's

Theater District. Before long, his practice was built up
by beautiful show girls—many of whom he also dated.

One morning in 1963 as he got ready for work and
viewed himself in the mirror, he saw "three chins."
Afterward, he got on the scales, which registered
225 pounds—many pounds up from his high school
weight of 135. He had lived on junk food during his
college and medical school years. Now it was time to
go on a diet and get the extra pounds off! None of the
diets he tried worked for very long, however, because
he would get incredibly hungry and start eating everything in sight. About this time, he read an article by
a Garfield Duncan, M.D., who advocated fasting and
getting into "Ketosis" to lose weight. Ketosis is a state
wherein so few carbohydrates are in the digestive system, the body is forced to burn its own fat for fuel.

About the same time, two Atlanta physicians, Walter Lyons Bloom and Gordon Azar, conducted a study
showing that ketosis could also be achieved by eating
protein and fat without carbohydrates. Atkins took
their findings to heart, along with British researchers,
Dr. A. Kekwick and Dr. G.L.S. Pawan, who found that
people who ate a diet of practically no carbohydrates
but up to 2,000 calories per day of fat and protein,
could still lose an abundance of weight. They lost as
much weight as those on a total fast in addition to not
experiencing hunger.

As time passed, Dr. Atkins' practice grew at a phenomenal rate—especially as show business people
came into his office. People, like Buddy Hackett, actor
and comedian, who lost over 100 pounds and Singer
Kaye Ballard, along with other celebrities. By September 1972, the hardcover edition of *Dr. Atkins' Diet Revolution* came off the press and four months after publication, a million copies were sold.

In addition to being a phenomenal new diet approach, the book set off a firestorm of criticism in the

medical community. All the well-known magazines in the U.S., like *Harper's Bazaar, Cosmopolitan, Mademoiselle,* and *Fortune,* ran stories and articles on the Atkins' Diet. Many new patients, even from far-flung corners of the earth flocked to Atkins' office and filled it to overflowing.

Although Atkins' unusual diet approach was praised by many people, it also received criticism from the medical community. It was branded as unhealthy because of its defiance of standard diets at the time. Dr. Atkins weathered the storm, however, sticking by his claims. In most cases he was able to back up his claims, too, but they were largely ignored by the medical community.

By the 1990's and beyond, however, because of the new recognition and acceptance of low-carb diets, Atkins began to receive his just due, and enjoyed popularity on the talk-show circuit. He remained a popular, though enigmatic figure until his sudden death after a fall on a slippery New York sidewalk when he injured his head (April 8, 2003). He had achieved a huge success at that point that many people could only dream of. That's the way he would have wanted his life to end—on a high note and by acceptance of the medical community as well as success and acceptance by the general public of his revolutionary weight-loss method.

Jean Nidetch, Founder of Weight Watchers (1923-?)

An ordinary Brooklyn, New York housewife, Jean Nidetch, started a multi-million dollar empire built on a weight-loss program.

Jean entered the world on Columbus Day (October 12), 1923, in Brooklyn, New York. At birth, Jean weighed a normal, 7 pounds 3 ounces. But as time passed, whenever she cried, her mother gave her something to eat—like a cookie or soda cracker. Of course, it wasn't long before she became a chubby little girl.

Jean's sister, Helen, was born when Jean was four. Jean's mother always introduced her children by addressing the "chubbiness": "This is Jean. She's always been chubby. And this is Helen, who wasn't chubby until after her operation."[24]

Growing up as a chubby (or fat) young girl intruded on Jean's life. Her weight was not only uncomfortable, but embarrassing as well. During a fire drill in elementary school, she said, "I was the last one to reach the cloak room...because it took forever to squeeze my fat little body out from behind my desk..." then "knocking over books, or maybe ink or another kid" on the way to the door.[24a] In high school, her life continued about the same as she sought out other overweight companions for eating and other activities.

After graduation, Jean got a job at the IRS. She liked the fact that the IRS gave its employees an abundance of coffee breaks. Whenever Jean had coffee, she had to have a Danish with it. In fact, she met Marty Nidetch in 1945 on one of her coffee breaks at a luncheonette across the street from the IRS. Marty had just returned from the army, was nice-looking and had a good sense of humor—and most important, Marty loved to eat. The two were married on April 20, 1947 after dating a couple of years.

Their marriage followed an interesting pattern as they sought out new eating places and eating places that offered "second helpings." Jean tried various crash diets, losing 20 to 30 pounds each time, but because of her eating habits, she always gained the weight back. She dieted for special occasions like birthdays or weddings. She ate things like eggs and grapefruit, or an oil and evaporated milk concoction that she drank three times a day. The drink made her constantly sick to her stomach, though, so she limited the times she went on it.

She and Marty moved different places for his job as a credit manager. One of the places they lived was Tulsa, Oklahoma where Jean got a job as a sales clerk. She turned out to be quite good at her job as she gave customers honest, candid answers to their questions. She would tell a prospective customer I don't think "it was for her"; but then I'd say, 'If you'll give me your phone number, I'll call you when something comes in that I think you'll like.'"[24b] Before long, Jean had a list of loyal clients who usually bought what she suggested. She admits to doubling her take home pay with her commissions.

The next job Marty had was in Warren, Pennsylvania as a store manager. Since the town was small and outside activities few, most of the entertaining was done at home. The Nidetch's fit right into the home entertaining situation and invited people into their home frequently serving snack items like cookies, crackers, and cakes. Since many of their friends and neighbors were overweight, no one seemed to notice that the Nidetchs were, too.

So, the weight kept piling on Jean's 5'7" frame. But she was becoming increasingly uncomfortable with the added pounds. Jean blamed her weight gain on happiness, or marriage, and on sadness after losing her first child. In 1951, she became pregnant again with her son, David. After his birth, she got in the habit of eating a snack every time she got up to feed him.

Before long, Marty and Jean realized they missed Brooklyn, so they moved back "home." While they were in Brooklyn, Jean became pregnant with their second son, Richard. But the doctors warned her about possible heart trouble if she didn't lose weight. She lost thirty pounds, but after the baby came, she gained it back by middle of the night snacking.

Finally, after becoming conscious of her overweight, unhealthy condition, Jean went to the New York City Board of Health Obesity Clinic. After a number of false starts and "cheating" on chocolate marshmallow cookies, she finally locked into the program and lost the recommended weight. To encourage herself and her overweight neighbors, she invited them into her home so they could talk about their eating problems.

As people lost weight, word got around about the Brooklyn housewife who had a diet plan that helped people get weight off. Everyone who came to the meetings at Jean's place admitted to having secret compulsions about food. The news about the meetings kept spreading around Brooklyn, then the state, and before long, all over the nation—and the world.

The H.J. Heinz Corporation bought the Weight Watchers Company in 1978. Jean Nidetch now lives in Florida, enjoying her family and many fond memories of how Weight Watchers changed her life for the better. She provides a great example of what one person can accomplish with will power and determination—even to changing the world—or at least a portion of it.

My Own Weight Loss Adventure

Even as I write this account, I'm in the process of losing weight. And, I'm succeeding on one of the two programs just mentioned. Right now, I want to lose about fifteen to twenty pounds. I've noticed even with the five or so pounds I've lost that climbing stairs is easier than it was. When a friend called me "Skinny Minnie" the other day, my motivation went through the roof!

Of course, not everyone needs to lose weight, but many Americans do. Our sedentary lifestyle means we don't use up the calories we did formerly, which causes our metabolism to slow down. If you need to lose weight, take heart, it's much easier and safer today than ever before. (Do check with your doctor before you start on any weight loss plan, though.) I wish you "BonVoyage" on your weight loss journey.

[23]*Dr. Robert Atkins: The True Story of the Man Behind the War on Carbohydrates.* Lisa Rogah. Penguin Group, New York, 2005, pp. 1, [23a]2, [23b]25, [23c]42.

[24]*The Jean Nidetch Story.* Weight Watchers International, New York City, N.Y.,1989, pp.13, [24a]13, [24b]21.

CHAPTER NINETEEN

GETTING REGULAR EXERCISE

"I Have to Get Off This Couch"

"The sovereign invigoration of the body is exercise, and of all exercises, walking is best."
Thomas Jefferson, Third U.S. President
(1743-1826)

Walking—the Easiest and Best Exercise

"Our lifestyles are killing us," so begins Casey Meyers' informative book on walking. The three leading causes of death in the U.S. are heart disease, cancer, and stroke. He also mentions "tobacco use" as being the leading cause of preventable deaths in the U.S. In fact, cigarette smoking accounts for 400,000 senseless deaths annually.

The second leading cause of death is "Poor diet, inactivity, and obesity." Statistical medical charts show a significant increase from 1990 to 2004, putting these causes of death only about two percent behind tobacco use.

Why are these diseases occurring so frequently? We can probably blame the advent of the automobile for much of this increase. The automobile has brought forth drive-ins of every kind, eliminating the need to walk even short distances: we now have drive-in banks, cleaners, pharmacies and last of all, fast food restaurants. The list of human energy savers goes on and on, including elevators, escalators, and even TV remote controls. In fact, much of what we do from the time we get up in the morning to the time we go to bed at night involves sitting. To reinforce this information, the American Heart Association gives these statistics in 2005: "Nearly seven of every 10 U.S. adults are overweight, and about three of every 10 are obese."[25]

Most likely each person reading these health statistics is somewhat aware of them already. So, let's talk about getting some type of mild exercise like walking. Of course, everyone knows how to walk—they've been walking from infancy.

My best advice if you're just starting a walking program is to walk where you live. To begin, you don't even have to walk fast, just be leisurely until your body gets used to walking regularly. Try for 15 to 20 minutes initially. Then, gradually increase your time to an hour. Wear comfortable, casual clothing and comfortable walking shoes (not running shoes, though), talk to a shoe salesman at an athletic shoe store; he can probably advise you about which shoes are best.

Before you begin each time, do some stretches that involve your ham string muscles. These exercises will prevent your getting stiff from walking by limbering up your muscles.

If you wish, you can walk with a buddy or in a small walking group. These groups often walk at malls, so check out a nearby mall and inquire about walking groups. You can also carry a small weight in each hand—from one and a half to two pounds—and swing your arms at the elbows as you walk. Carrying these weights will exercise your arms as well as your legs.

The good thing about walking for exercise is that you can walk anywhere. In fact, try to use small increments of time to walk, even parking your car some distance from the shopping center so you have further to walk. I live on the second floor, a decision I made when I moved here. I wanted to climb two flights of stairs to give me more exercise. Try to work up to walking at least three times a week for maximum health benefits. After that, the sky's the limit. Increase your walking as much as you wish. You'll have more energy and keep your weight under control.

If you can't walk, try using a recumbent bike or swimming for exercise. Whatever you do, for your heart's sake find some form of exercise that you enjoy. Before long, you'll feel so much better, stronger, and have more energy. So, for your health's sake—you'll be glad you did!

The Highlight of my Running Career

Talking with my older brother, Ken, a physician and world-class runner, I was persuaded to run in the Emily Midas 6.2 mile race in Detroit one year. The race took place in July, and I dressed in a cool white and green shirt and matching shorts.

As we prepared to drive to the starting point, Ken said, "Hurry up, Bonnie, we don't want to be late." I was nearly ready, but my nerves weren't. Ken reassured me and his wife, Barb, by telling us, "I'm not going to run too fast. I'll wait for the two of you." So that's what happened. We got to the race site just before the race started. Hundreds of people were ready to run and each of us received a number. A band played lively music and the air was charged with electricity.

I wasn't used to running 6.2 miles, but I did it because my "big" brother spurred me on. When we got back home after the race, I had blisters on both feet. But my brother doctored my blisters as he had said earlier—and I had the satisfaction when I went to bed that night of knowing I had pleased him. Sad to say, though, the great running career Ken envisioned for me following the race never materialized. Guess I "peaked out" running the Emily Midas Race that hot July Day in Detroit some years ago.

"Exercise daily in God—no spiritual flabbiness, please! Workouts in the gymnasium are useful, but a disciplined life in God is far more so, making you fit both today and forever. You can count on this, take it to heart."

2 Timothy 4:17 (*The Message Bible*)

[25]*Walking: A Complete Guide to the Complete Exercise.* Casey Meyers. Ballantine Books (Trade Paperback Edition), 2007.

CHAPTER TWENTY

MAINTAINING A POSITIVE OUTLOOK

"This Could Be So Much Worse"

"Faith begins as a thin trickle across the mind. Repeated, it becomes habitual. It cuts into the consciousness until, as you deepen the channel, faith-thought overflows and whatever you think about the world becomes optimistic and positive.

To be efficient in prayer you must learn the art of praying. You can read every book ever written about prayer, and you can attend innumerable discussions on prayer, but the only way to pray is to pray.

Make your prayers simple and natural...talk to God as to a friend."

Norman Vincent Peale (1898-1993)

Norman Vincent Peale, Advocate of Positive Thinking (1898-1993)

"With his charming accessibility, good humor, and matchless style as a story teller," Norman Vincent Peale could captivate almost any audience.[26] His charm and message arrived on the American scene following "the Great Depression" and just before World War II began. Americans needed some new hope and optimism to carry them through this uncertain time.

The timing of Norman Vincent Peale's birth appeared perfect for the task given to him. Norman arrived in the home of Anna and Clifford Peale on May 31, 1898 in the small Ohio town of Bowersville. Although Clifford was a Methodist minister, he had earlier trained to become a medical doctor, so he and Anna decided to deliver their own first born without the benefit of other helping personnel.

By the time Norman was 17 and ready for college, he had lived in seven Ohio locations and more than a dozen Methodist parsonages because of his father's call to different churches as a Methodist minister.

The Peale family moved to yet another church in Greenville, Ohio, when Norman was twelve. When they moved three years later, he turned fifteen. In spite of his many moves, young Norman finished the full high school curriculum, including courses in Latin, German, the usual English, history, math, and science in 1916 from Belle Fontaine High School. During this time he picked up part-time jobs like delivering newspapers and even a job as a door-to-door salesman.

Every summer, Norman attended the Methodist Camp meeting center in Lakeside, Ohio. The Peale Family was at the camp meeting when news came about the beginning of World War I. The year included the news that the State of Ohio defeated Prohibition by an 83,000 vote majority.

Norman began his college career in 1916 at Ohio Wesleyan, a Methodist institution where he received scholarship help. Ohio Wesleyan was a thorough-going Methodist school that prohibited smoking, drinking, and dancing and required weekday chapel attendance and Sunday church attendance.

A somewhat difficult time for Peale came as he continued to struggle with reciting in class. A kind teacher, Professor Arneson, kept him after class one day and gave him two suggestions: 1) to ask Jesus to help him (with his inferiority complex), and 2) to look up the writings of American psychologist, William James. Norman followed through with his professor's advice and was greatly helped.

Some of Norman's professors, like his English professor, tended to emphasize the ideas and teaching of Ralph Waldo Emerson and psychologist William James, as well. Later on, Norman would incorporate some of their teachings in his own theology and Sunday sermons.

Peale had already enrolled at Boston University following his undergraduate graduation. He signed up to earn a master's degree in literature but also left room for theology classes. Before he completed his first year, however, he transferred to the Boston University School of Theology after receiving a "call" to the ministry.

By the time he graduated from the seminary, Peale found himself in the midst of the "Roaring Twenties" with all the decade's optimism—despite prohibition being the law of the land. Much was changing in the country, including the role of religion in people's lives. The social gospel became more and more accepted, although Norman disdained it since he was a solid evangelical. He was called to his first church in Brooklyn, New York to King's Highway Methodist Church. The new minister would have a lot to work with given the great population increase. People from the city began to come to the area of King's Highway Methodist Church—30,000 newcomers between 1921 and 1924.

Norman threw himself into his work. Being unmarried, he could donate his time to increasing church membership and building the church. His messages centered around having a friendly relationship with Jesus, although the services themselves were more formal with lofty, semi-classical music.

Then, in April 1927, Norman was invited to preach at University Avenue Methodist Church in Syracuse, New York. Within the month, he was asked to become the church's new pastor. He titled his first sermon, "The Glory of the Future," using the tenth chapter of John's Gospel as his text.

The church was located next to Syracuse University, a Methodist school with a few thousand students. Peale believed the established church had an important role to play in contemporary culture. In fact, he told his Syracuse congregation: "Only the Christian church can keep alive free institutions, the rights of man, and the sacredness of personality."[26a]

Norman's overall message was still taking shape at this time. In a sermon at University Church near the end of the 1920's, he told his congregation about two "Positive Thinkers": One was the Apostle Peter, the other was arctic explorer Richard Byrd. He claimed the goals they achieved were provided by inner qualities available to everyone; in fact, he suggested heroic accomplishments came from "harmonizing life with the Spirit of Christ."[26b] In addition, he confirmed, their achievements were not extraordinary, for "given a normal intelligence, an individual can make of himself about what he wants to do."[26c]

Norman also called Jesus' Sermon on the Mount in Matthew's gospel, a "practical program for personality building."[26d] The majority of his sermons now focused on problems of daily living, although at this time the messages weren't concerned with technique. Membership at the church continued to grow during these years, even during the years of the stock market crash membership mushroomed.

A newspaper reported of Peale at this time in the early 1930's that "he regularly preached to over a thousand at University Church and ventured that he was one of the most eloquent and attractive speakers in the state. He possessed an uncanny ability to understand the existential moment, to sense an audience and sculpt his message to its sensibilities; he had the intuitive skills of a populist, now honed by experience. Audiences didn't like him, they loved him."[26e]

On June 20, 1930, Norman Vincent Peale and Ruth Stafford were married. The two seemed extraordinarily compatible and their marriage lasted over sixty years. Ruth had been a student at Syracuse University and was eight years younger than Peale.

Then, in March 1932, Norman received calls from two churches: First Methodist Church in Los Angeles and Marble Collegiate in New York City. Although the California church had over 7,000 members, Marble Collegiate was better endowed, as well as being an old, historic church. Finally, Peale decided on Marble Collegiate where he remained throughout his long ministry until he retired in 1984.

Some of the other endeavors of Peale were his writing career and his speaking career. Pastoring at Marble Collegiate gave him the freedom to pursue these activities. He instituted a "healing" clinic to encourage those individuals hit hard by the depression, *Guideposts Magazine*, the book, and *The Power of Positive Thinking*, which sold at least six million copies from its first publishing date in 1952. Probably Peale's advice to his constituents and many others to remain positive about their situation is good advice—advice that he himself followed despite some of life's seeming paradoxes along the way.

Prayer
"In the morning, prayer is the key that opens to us the treasures of God's mercies and blessings. In the evening, it is the key that shuts us up under his protection and safeguard."

Anonymous

Answers

With a reduced income after my husband's death, I prayed much about paying the rent. After I'd prayed for some time, the phone rang one morning, and I recognized the voice on the other end as the office manager of the apartments where I lived. She said, "An elderly lady needs a downstairs apartment and her family will pay someone two and one half months' rent to move." I asked her how soon the apartment was needed, she answered, "Immediately."

Since it was already November, I had no time to lose to get everything packed once I agreed to the arrangement. I contacted the "Bull Dog" Movers, and they said they'd move me from the downstairs apartment to the upstairs one for $300, but that everything, except the furniture, would need to be in boxes.

The move turned out to be more difficult than I thought, but thanks to some kind-hearted friends, Bill and Ileen Daly, everything got boxed up and ready to move on Monday morning after Thanksgiving. Of course, it took awhile to get settled in my new place, but I still love the view overlooking trees from the Sun Room windows. I call my apartment my "tree house." And the elderly lady's family did pay me two and a half months rent to move—one of the more interesting answers to prayer I've had!

[26]*God's Salesman.* Carol V.R. George. Oxford University Press, 1993, pp. 15, [26a]61, [26b]62, [26c]63, 63, [26d]63, [26e]66.

CHAPTER TWENTY-ONE

REACHING OUT TO OTHERS

"Someone may need my help"

"The slightest misstep brought a torrent of groans from some poor, mangled fellow in your path."

Clara Barton (1821-1912)

Clara Barton, Civil War Hero, American Red Cross Founder

Small of stature and patriotic from an early age, Clarissa Harlowe Barton (Clara) was born on December 25, 1821, in North Oxford, Massachusetts. Her parents, Stephen Barton and Sarah Stone Barton, already had four children: Dorothy (Dolly), age 17, Stephen, age 15, David, age 13, and Sally, age 10.

From a young child, Clara enjoyed sitting on her "soldier father's" lap listening to his stories of war. Through these stories she learned much about military strategy and tactics. Her father, a successful farmer, horse breeder, and local politician, sometimes moderated town meetings. He gave money regularly to help the poor and even used his own money to establish a home for the poor. Earlier in his life he had been a soldier and fought against American Indians with future U.S. President William Henry Harrison. He was present during the war of 1812 when the great Shawnee leader, Tecumseh, was killed.

Because of her father's influence, Clara said, "I early learned that next to Heaven, our highest duty was to love and serve our country, and honor and support its laws."[27] On the other hand, Clara's mother taught the young girl many useful household skills like sewing, cooking, gardening, weaving cloth, canning fruit, and milking cows. Clara's mother, a plain hard-working woman, saw no need for her daughter to have dolls or toys. Instead, Clara worked alongside her sisters doing household chores and learned not to complain or fuss.

Clara also learned many useful things from her siblings. Her sister, Dolly, already a teacher when Clara was born, helped care for her little sister. Her brother, Stephen, too, was already a teacher at the time of her birth, but took over his father's textile mill a few years later. Stephen, a gifted mathematician, taught Clara arithmetic on her little slate.

Even her older brother, David, contributed to her education. David loved animals and the outdoors. He was patient with his little sister and taught her to pound a nail with a hammer and throw a ball like a boy. One of the important things David taught Clara, however, was to ride horses bareback. At age five, Clara learned to hang on tight to the horse's mane. This skill saved her life several times when she needed to flee from an approaching Confederate Army. Although years older, the sibling closest in age to Clara was Sally. She introduced Clara to literature and poetry.

When Clara turned four, she went to a two-term school session each of which lasted three months. Her teacher, Colonel Richard C. Stone, asked her to spell cat and dog—but she said she could spell "artichoke." Mr. Stone then placed her in an advanced reading class.

In 1829, Clara's parents sent her to boarding school, but she was miserable and stopped eating so her teacher and the local doctor sent her home. By this time, her parents had bought a 300-acre farm. Clara and her four cousins—the Learneds—enjoyed playing in the wide-open spaces on the farm.

When Clara was eleven, her brother David fell from the top of a barn he was helping to build. So Clara quit school to stay home and care for him. She even applied loathsome leeches to drain off excess blood from his body. Later, a doctor advocated a steam-bath cure. That suggestion put an end to the leeches and David made a full recovery within three weeks.

Following David's recovery, thirteen-year-old Clara returned to her studies. Her teacher, Lucien Burleigh, gave her instruction in history, languages, English literature, and composition. The next year her teacher was Jonathon Dana; he gave her lessons in advanced philosophy, chemistry, and Latin. All Clara's teachers marveled at her diligence in studying and at her thirst for knowledge.

When school was out, Clara worked at her brother Stephen's mill. Since she was small, Stephen had to build a special little platform for his sister to stand on. She worked there only two weeks, however, when the mill burned to the ground.

Clara Barton, School Teacher

At the age of eighteen, Clara began teaching school. She had forty students and wore a new green dress designed to make her look older. The young teacher was nervous as she stood in front of her class, made up of young children to boys a few years younger than she.

At recess, Clara joined the rowdier, older boys and participated in their sports and showed her athletic ability. "My four lads soon perceived that I was no stranger to their sports or their tricks."[27a] Her students awarded her "high marks" for her ability.

Everywhere she taught, Clara not only disciplined her students but taught them as well. When she was assigned to a school at Millward, however, Clara almost met her match. She tried at first to win over her students with smiles and kindness. But some of the bigger boys continued to disrupt the classroom. The ringleader of the disruptive group came to class late one morning. When he came in, he mocked Clara and upset the class, so Clara retrieved a riding whip from her desk, asked him to step forward and lashed him with the whip. She shocked the entire class with her actions. The young man stood up and apologized to his teacher. From then on, Clara was given problem schools to teach in; in general, she managed to discipline her students and still teach them the "three R's."

Her next venture was to teach at a public school in New Jersey where none had existed. Her school opened with six students to 600 a year later. But the school board demoted her to being only a school mistress, and they placed a man in charge of running the school. The demotion devastated Barton since she had developed and run the school for two years, then to have the board put a man in charge of the school because she was a mere woman. A short time later when she had an ailment of her vocal chords, she resigned teaching, never to teach again.

On to Washington, D.C

In 1854, Clara moved to Washington, D.C. She hoped the milder climate would help her voice, and she ended up spending the next 60 years of her life in the city. Through Colonel Alexander Dewitt, a congressman and distant cousin from her home district, she found work in the Patent Office under Judge Charles Mason, the Commissioner of Patents. Most of the clerks were men, but Mason recognized Clara's superb work ethics and her fine handwriting. Clara became the first woman to work full time in the Patent Office. Before long, Mason promoted Clara to a position at the Confidential desk overseeing secret documents. Mason paid her the same salary as the men: $1400 per year—quite a lot of money at the time, especially for a woman. Some of the men were jealous of her and accused her falsely, but Mason put an end to it, firing the men.

Times began to change in Washington and in the entire nation as tempers flared and fights even broke out between slavery and anti-slavery forces. When Abraham Lincoln was elected president in 1860 (1861), Clara Barton already had a good friend in Congress, Senator Henry Wilson, who would be much help to her later on. Lincoln even appointed Wilson Chairman of the Committee on Military Affairs.

War

Then, on April 12, 1861, when the south fired on Fort Sumter, the President declared war and asked for 75,000 soldiers to defend Washington, D.C. from rebels. Neighborhood groups of volunteer soldiers and militia arrived in Washington a few days later in response to Lincoln's summons. Included in the troops were forty young men in the Sixth Massachusetts Regiment who were former students of Clara Barton's. A short time later, as she tended wounded soldiers, Barton remarked in a letter to a friend, "So far as our poor efforts can reach, they shall never lack a kindly hand or a sister's sympathy if they come. In my opinion, this city will be attacked within the next sixty days...and when there is no longer a soldier's arm to raise the stars and stripes above our capitol, may God give strength to mine."[27b]

Clara's relief efforts to the troops started soon after the influx of all the volunteers coming into Washington. Before long, she collected goods from churches, families and other groups. Her rented quarters in Washington began to overflow with clothing, bandages, jellies, liquors, preserves, medicines, and other supplies. Finally, she rented a warehouse, eventually filling three warehouses with supplies. Clara's sister, Sally, came to help her tend the wounded men near the capitol.

To the Front

After the Battle of Fair Oaks on May 11, 1862, Barton learned of the 8,000 men wounded from the battle. She soon quit her job at the Patent Office to better serve the troops. When she met with Colonel Daniel H. Rucker, assistant quartermaster general in charge of transportation, he gave her permission to have six wagons loaded with men and supplies to move to the front.

When she gathered all the necessary permits and passes, Clara was ready to travel to the battlefield. She wore a long, dark skirt, a plaid jacket and a kerchief over her hair. She arrived at Culpepper, Virginia, two days after the Battle of Cedar Mountain on August 9, 1862. As her wagon came to the field hospital at midnight, Brigade Surgeon James L. Dunn was amazed to discover that Clara had brought bandages, dressings, and other supplies—all items the hospital had run out of. Dunn praised her, referring to her as an "angel sent from heaven."

As she ministered to the troops missing arms and legs, she gave them applesauce, soup, and bread soaked in wine. Other organizations had by this time been raised up to tend the wounded and dying men. After each battle when Clara's supplies were exhausted, she returned to the city to restock her supplies. Over and over Barton ministered to the wounded soldiers during the days of the war. She received much praise for her timely help and work following the war's major battles.

After Robert E. Lee surrendered at Appomattox on April 12, 1865, Clara found a new job. Under the authority of President Lincoln, she began to search for some 80,000 missing soldiers. Clara's forte' was setting up and organizing records, which she did.

Following her duties of locating missing soldiers, Barton began a series of lectures recounting her civil war experiences. She earned $75 to $100 for each lecture, taking in as much as $1000 some months. She needed the money since she had exhausted her own savings on provisions for the soldiers for whom she cared. Clara's lecture tour, although bringing in much needed monies, left her exhausted. Her doctor recommended a trip to Europe for rest and relaxation. She travelled with her sister Sally, at first to Glasgow, Scotland. From there, Clara went to Geneva, Switzerland, where she was approved by a group of Swiss dignitaries, including Doctor Louis Appia, who participated in establishing the International Red Cross.

After some time, during which Barton helped war victims in Europe, Clara returned to America where her doctor again prescribed rest. In the meantime, however, she was persuaded by Dr. Louis Appia to head up the International Red Cross in America. And, by May 21, 1881, after negotiations were completed with government officials, the American Red Cross was formed with Clara Barton as President at age sixty.

Clara Barton's contributions to her country proved to be great. Her heroism during the civil war in reaching out to the dead and dying soldiers received much praise not only from officials above her, but from the soldiers to whom she ministered.

Her heroism also extended to founding the American Red Cross—surely this last, is a tribute to her courage and mercy to those suffering in time of war and tragedy. Truly, Clara Barton's legacy lives on during every kind of crisis in the U.S. when the Red Cross comes on the scene. Were she alive today, she would rejoice in what her vision has wrought.

Help in Time of Need

Each of us has times when we need a helping hand. For me, this time came when my baby was one week old. My husband Ray and I and our firstborn child, a healthy blonde, blue-eyed baby girl we named Cynthia (Cindy) were newcomers to the Chicago area; so we didn't actually know anyone that hot month of August some years ago. As we brought the baby home, everything seemed fine. We stopped enroute to our modest home to pick up a few necessary items for the baby.

After a few days, however, I developed an infection and a high fever of 102 degrees. I could no longer care for the baby and my distraught husband didn't know where to turn until a kind neighbor, a registered nurse, offered to take the baby to her home and care for her a few days.

As the anti-biotic did its work in me along with the rest, I quickly recovered and was able within three or four days to care for my baby. But if Nurse Jane hadn't offered her services, I'm not sure what we'd have done. Certainly, Jane was an "angel of mercy" to my husband and me at that time.

As I have opportunity to reach out to others since then, I try to do so. Even in small ways, we can help each other—things like carrying a package, holding a door open, or even giving someone a friendly smile. Whatever we do for others always comes back to us as we apply the "Golden Rule."

[27]*Clara Barton*. Susan E. Hamen. ABDO Publishing Company, Edina, MN, 2010, pp. 17, [27a]29, [27b]43.

CHAPTER TWENTY-TWO

REDISCOVERING YOURSELF

"There's more to me than I thought"

"A man of genius makes no mistakes. His errors are volitional and are the portals of discovery."

James Joyce (1882-1941)

Andrew Carnegie, Self-taught Steel Magnate (1835-1919)

Andrew Carnegie's ancestral roots were in Dunfermline, Scotland, where he was born on November 25, 1835. His father, William, was a weaver, working his craft many hours a day on the first floor of the family home. His mother, Margaret Morrison Carnegie, helped her husband by keeping him supplied with spools of yarn that were constantly being unwound by the loom. In addition to helping her husband, Andrew's mother cooked, sewed, laundered, and managed the household. She also brought in water from fountains, pumps, or wells, and gathered wood, charcoal, and coal from nearby sources.

Life was not easy for the Carnegies, although they were somewhat better off than the majority of their neighbors. Dunfermline had numerous cottages, all looking alike, built with gray stone and having two stories—like the Carnegie house. Situated in East-central

Scotland, somewhat north of Edinburgh, Scotland's capital, Dunfermline had a renowned history. In fact, many of the kings, queens, and princes of early Scotland were born, lived or were buried here.

Both of Andrew's parents were unusual in that they read newspapers and other materials to stay abreast of the political and current events of the day. His parents even broke away from the traditional church of the day, the Presbyterian church, and embraced other faiths—his mother, the Unitarian, his father, Swedenborgianism.

By the time Andrew turned eight, two major changes occurred in his life: his brother, Thomas, was born, and the young boy realized his mother could no longer give him her full attention, so he started to school. Later, he claimed his parents waited until he wanted to go to school.

The school Andrew attended was very formal, and the school master sat on a small raised platform at the front of the classroom. A leather strap lay beside him, which he applied to any boy who misbehaved. But Andrew loved school and seldom had the strap applied to him.

Everything changed for the Carnegie family when the looms in Scotland began to operate by steam. Andrew's father couldn't compete with the steam-powered looms and the family began a descent into poverty. Andrew's mother knew then it was time to emigrate to the United States.

When the Carnegies arrived in the United States, they went to Pittsburgh, Pennsylvania, located at the point where the Monongahela and Allegheny Rivers meet to form the Ohio River. Pittsburgh was little more than a frontier town in 1848. The Carnegies soon settled in with relatives already living in the area.

William Carnegie set up a loom to weave homespun checkered tablecloths then popular, but he could not compete with the steam-powered looms in price and efficiency. So both father and son began working at a neighborhood mill, which was hard work, but at least they had jobs.

Now Andrew began a rapid rise to success because of his diligent work habits and his intelligence. He left the factory job and became a "bobbin boy" at another location. A year later, he procured a job as a telegraph messenger boy at two and a half dollars a week, which was a 100 percent increase from where he started at his earlier job.

At his messenger boy job, Andrew didn't realize that being involved with the telegraph he was affiliated with the latest technology of the time. Nevertheless, he liked this job and later wrote, "From a dark cellar running a steam engine, begrimed with coal dirt without a trace of the elevating traces of life, I was lifted into Paradise, yes, Heaven it seemed to me, with newspapers, pens, pencils, and sunshine about me."[28]

Andy Carnegie soon became well known in downtown Pittsburgh as he memorized not only the street names and the city layout, but business people's names as well. And, as the new telegraph service flourished in Pittsburgh, so did Andy.

One day the superintendent of the telegraph service visited the office, now consisting of five young men, all of Scottish descent. He saw the boys in their rough street clothes and decided the company needed a better image, so he sent all of them to a tailor to be fitted with sharp, dark-green uniforms.

While Andrew worked as a messenger boy, a Colonel James Anderson opened his library to working boys and allowed them to check out one book a week. Andy never missed a week checking out books. In his spare time at the telegraph office, Andrew learned telegraphy, and a short time later, he became a telegraph operator at seventeen, earning $25 a month. He worked at the telegraph company as a clerk and telegrapher for the Pittsburgh division of the Pennsylvania Railroad. One day an accident occurred tying up the entire division while T.A. Scott, the division superintendent, was out on the line and unreachable. Andy took matters into his own hands and kept things moving on the line by issuing orders and signing them, T.A. Scott. From that time on, Andy practically ran the entire division.

One day Superintendent Scott asked him, "Andy, can you find $500 to invest?"[29] Truthfully, about all young Carnegie had was 500 cents, but he asked for more information. Scott told him about a station agent who wanted to sell ten shares of Adams Express for $500. Scott said it was a good opportunity.

Andrew talked things over with his resourceful mother that evening, and she decided to borrow $500 from a relative using the house as collateral. A month later, Andrew received an envelope addressed to: Andrew Carnegie, Esquire that contained a dividend check for $10. Andrew was thrilled with the idea of investing money, not working for it, and receiving the reward from it. Soon, another opportunity came to Andrew. A man came to him asking his opinion about a "sleeping car" idea he had. The man was T.T. Woodruff, inventor of the railroad sleeping car.

Success followed success for Carnegie, and before long he invested in the oil fields of Pennsylvania. In 1864 he realized that the country's railroads needed much repair, so he began to manufacture iron rails. In addition, he formed the Keystone Bridge Company, calling for the construction of iron railroad bridges to span the rivers.

Carnegie, a small man only five feet, four inches tall, had a genius for handling situations and men. He soon met with George Pullman to consolidate their rival sleeping car companies. Before long, the Pullman

Palace Car Company had a worldwide monopoly on sleeping cars.

Carnegie next invested in an oil field in Pennsylvania. He invested during the time of the civil war, and no one could foresee the use of oil at that time. But he took a risk in his investment, not the first, nor the last. Carnegie always seemed to be in the right place at the right time to get in on a profitable venture.

In 1866, Carnegie decided to put his businesses on hold and take an extended European trip. He and two friends sailed for Europe visiting all the great cities like Amsterdam, London, Paris, and Berlin. For nine months they traveled by train, ship and horse-drawn carriages.

Upon his return to the United States in late 1866, Carnegie, age 31, plunged back into his work. In each of his investments, he tried to keep in touch with the company and not let it exist without his input. He also knew he needed more capital to manage his investments. He realized, too, that he needed to go to New York City to find the needed finances. So in 1867, Andy moved to New York City along with his mother. The Carnegies rented rooms in what was the finest hotel in America, the St. Nicholas Hotel in lower Manhattan.

New York City seemed to be waiting for Andrew Carnegie. He already had a good reputation in a few business circles, and he set about widening those circles. He was known for his boundless energy, good humor, plain speech, honesty, and his genius for dealing with all types of people. His connection with the British also helped him gain the confidence of investors.

By 1874, following the financial panic of the previous year, Carnegie bought out his competitors in the steel business. At that time he dominated the steel business until Charles Schwab, Elbert H. Gary, and J. Pierpont Morgan discussed a plan for a billion dollar company to dominate the steel business of the world.

They asked Carnegie if he would sell his business; he said, "Yes," and named his price. Although they fumed about it, they finally gave in to Carnegie, who received $490,000,000 in bonds, preferred stock, and in common stock.

After completing the deal, Carnegie announced to the world that he considered it a disgrace to die rich and didn't intend to be disgraced. Thus, he donated a $5,000,000 fund to the men of his mills; he started library gifts with five and a quarter million dollars for sixty-eight branch libraries in New York City; he gave $28,000,000 to the Carnegie Institute in Pittsburgh; $25,000,000 to the Carnegie Institute in Washington, organized to assist any activity for the Carnegie Hero Fund, and gave additional monies away for worthy causes. When Carnegie died in 1919 at age 84, he had given away over $300,000,000. He was left with a modest estate of $30,000,000. But in addition, many small towns across the U.S. benefitted from Carnegie Libraries—the remarkable legacy of a remarkable man who rediscovered himself in a new world.

Returning to School

Starting college at any age can be formidable, but to go back as an adult with twenty-year-old classmates can be frightening. However, that's what I did after several years of marriage.

My first class was a "Survey of European Literature" course taught by Dr. Thurston, a graduate teaching assistant. Approximately 100 students were in the class, so I was just a number. But the professor was good and made everything we studied such as *The Iliad* and *The Odyssey* interesting. He made the works we studied so contemporary.

I had adjusted to the class fairly well, but then came our first exam. I was petrified! Here I had my long-awaited opportunity of going to college and I might blow it if I failed the exam. I did the best I could on the essay-type exam, handed my paper in and left the classroom.

A few weeks passed and still the papers weren't returned. Then, one day I ran a little late for class and came in as Dr. Thurston read from one of the exam papers. A student next to me said, "Listen to all the 'corny' stuff and clichés on that paper. That's not what I consider good writing!"

At that point I realized the professor was reading my paper and commenting on it. Soon, as the papers were handed back I glanced at my fellow student's paper—it had a big red "C" on it. Then I received my paper back. I had a red "A" and "Well done!" on it.

So I got an "A" on the paper and for my first return to college class. What an encouragement. I was off and running toward my goal of becoming a college graduate and entering a whole new world.

[28]*Andrew Carnegie.* John S. Bowman. Silver Burdett Press, Simon & Schuster, 1989, p. 28.

[29]*Investing: Famous Fortunes.* Books for Libraries Press, 1931, p. 131.

CHAPTER TWENTY-THREE

LEARNING NEW SKILLS AND NEW THINGS

"I haven't tried that before"

"How happy is he born and taught,
That serveth not another's will;
Whose armor is his honest thought,
And simple truth his utmost skill."
"The Character of a Happy Life"
Sir Henry Wooten (1568-1639)

Daniel Boone, Wilderness Pioneer (1734-1820)

One of the earliest and most famous frontiersmen in the United States was Daniel Boone. Daniel first appeared in Berks County, Pennsylvania on November 2, 1734, the sixth child of Squire Boone and his wife's eleven children.

Squire Boone was a Quaker and married a Quaker woman by the name of Sarah Morgan. Squire also worked as a weaver, weaving wool, cotton, or linen, on a loom. By the time Daniel was born, his father had also set up a blacksmith's shop on his twenty-five acre homestead and he grazed cattle.

Daniel, however, didn't care much for farming. His interests lay in the woods that surrounded the Boone property. He spent every spare minute exploring the outdoors. Because of his love of the outdoors, Daniel didn't spend much time in school; however, his knowledge of life in the woods was vast.

When he was a teenager, he had become an excellent shot with a rifle to the point he repaired guns in his father's blacksmith shop and supplied wild game for the Boone dinner table.

From the time of his youth, Daniel displayed much daring. This characteristic stayed with him throughout his life. He also refused to back down from a fight, causing some dissension with other Quakers who were pacifists. Daniel's whole family agreed with Daniel about the restrictiveness of Quaker life. This disagreement with the Quakers resulted in their moving from Pennsylvania to North Carolina in 1748. In their new state they set up another homestead near the Yadkin River just on the edge of the frontier. The Boones were now in Indian territory belonging to the Cherokees and the Shawnees. Each of these tribes could attack at any time when threatened. Historian John Bakeless has suggested about the Boones: "The Boones were wanderers born. They had the itching foot....They heard of distant lands and knew that they must go there."[30]

As a young boy, Daniel made friends with the Indians and studied their ways. At the age of ten, Daniel's father bought twenty-five acres of wooded pasture. The land was some miles from the main farm, and Daniel spent the following six summers there with his mother where they tended the cattle. His father stayed home and managed the loom and blacksmith shop. Daniel's oldest sister took care of the younger children.

Daniel roamed the woods during the day while the cattle grazed, and at night he drove them home for milking. At thirteen, Daniel's father gave him a short-barreled, muzzle-loading rifle. Before long, he turned into an excellent marksman. He hunted deer, turkey, and bears with his (at that time) long-barreled flintlock. He could, according to legend, shoot a tick off a bear's snout at one hundred yards. Sometimes he stayed in the woods for weeks at a time. On the frontier, pioneers considered this time a "long hunt." Daniel returned with abundant hides and furs, which made a profitable sale.

In 1754, British and French forces clashed on the western frontier. The first shots fired signaled the beginning of the French and Indian War. Not long after the outbreak of this war, Daniel met Rebecca Bryant and married her on August 14, 1756. The newlyweds moved into a cabin on Sugar Creek.

Before long, however, Daniel grew restless and wanted to leave because of settlers moving into the area and killing off the abundant game. But Rebecca refused, not wanting to leave family and friends. As it turned out, John Finley stopped by the Boone cabin in 1769. Finley had told Daniel earlier about the paradise of Kentucky.

So, on May 1, Daniel led Finley and four friends westward. The men journeyed through the Cumberland Gap on a Native American Trail called "The Warrior's Trace." Within a few weeks, Daniel stood atop a hill north of the Kentucky River. There, for the first time, he gazed at "The beautiful {land} of Kentucky." [30a]

The Iroquois named the area "K a n t a-ke," meaning "meadows." Boone was not the first to see these bluegrass meadows. The Shawnee, Cherokee, and other tribes had blazed trails through the area for decades. For six months, Daniel's party hunted deer and trapped beaver.

But one day a Shawnee war party cornered Daniel and John Stevens, his brother-in-law. They took all the hides, plus the horses, but soon released the captives. It became a game as Daniel and John quickly recaptured the goods with the Shawnees taking them back. Ultimately, Boone and his brother-in-law escaped and had to begin trapping all over again.

By the time Daniel returned home, he was empty handed; another war party had stolen his goods. Now, he was in debt. While in Kentucky, however, Daniel had studied the location of each hill, stream, and salt lick.

But now, Americans were pushing beyond the mountains, and in 1773, a wealthy Virginia landowner named William Russell wanted to explore Kentucky. He chose Daniel to lead his expedition. The expedition ended badly when a Delaware war party descended on the supply train headed up by James Boone, Daniel's sixteen-year-old son. The warriors killed Boone and his friend, Henry Russell.

The entire expedition lost heart and returned home. Daniel had to hunt all winter to feed his family. Daniel was now promoted to Militia Lieutenant, taking charge of several frontier forts. When the fighting ended with the Native Americans, Daniel was promoted to Captain.

Sometime later, Daniel and a number of workmen began to build a road into the Kentucky wilderness. The land lay between the Kentucky and Cumberland Rivers. On April 6, 1775, the road was finished, although most of the time it "was hilly, stony, or muddy."[30b]

Daniel spent the rest of his days involved in many different exploits. He was heralded by the settlers' communities for his daring and for his craftiness in the woods. He was also respected by many Native Americans, like Blackfish, of the Shawnees, for his courage.

He sold off much of his land in order to be debt free. As he told his children, "He would rather be poor than retain an acre of land...so long as claims and debts hung over him."[30c] Boone died on September 26, 1820 in his mid-eighties following a brief illness; but the stories and legends about him continue to grow until it becomes difficult to separate fact from fiction. Nevertheless, Boone's skills in the wilderness helped pave the way for the westward move of the settlers in the U.S. Without his skills, the frontier would have taken much longer to accomplish.

Taking Pictures

A few years ago, my husband and I planned a trip to England. I was so excited and in preparation for the trip, I decided to sign up for a non-credit photography class at a local school.

I had an old, but good, 30-millimeter Japanese camera. I took it to class each time with eager anticipation. I planned on taking pictures of Buckingham Palace, The Tower of London, and other British landmarks. *My pictures would rival Ansell Adams' any day,* I thought, as I snapped pictures of interesting tree trunks and stray cats and dogs entering the back yard. I learned about proportion and perspective and other necessary facts about photography in class, so I was ready.

The day came when we packed our belongings and prepared to leave for London. My husband asked, "Did you get plenty of film for the camera?"

"Yes," I replied, happily. "I got at least six rolls. That should be sufficient." I was anxious to show off my new photography skills—having everything in the photos just right—no cut off people's legs, etc.

Soon we flew across the Atlantic, arriving at our destination in the evening and on to our hotel (after an eight-hour flight). Day after day, I diligently snapped pictures of tourist attractions in London: Trafalgar Square, the Changing of the Guard, and Westminster Abbey.

After our arrival back home, however, I discovered with keen disappointment, that none of the pictures turned out—the film had not been properly inserted into the camera.

That ended my pursuit of photography. Ansell Adams, you can keep your crown!

[30]*Daniel Boone: Wilderness Pioneer.* Wm. R. Sanford & Carl R. Green. Enslow Publishers, Springfield, N.J., 1997, pp. 9, [30a]17, [30b]24, [30c]36.

CHAPTER TWENTY-FOUR

GROWING MENTALLY, EMOTIONALLY, AND SPIRITUALLY

"There's much I can learn through all this"

"I went to the woods because I wished to live deliberately, to front only the essential facts of life, and see if I could not learn what it had to teach, and not, when I came to die discover that I had not lived."

Henry David Thoreau (1817-1862)

George Washington Carver, Botanist and Inventor (1864-1943)

In 1864, George Carver experienced a tumultuous beginning: when he was just a few weeks old, he and his mother, Mary, were kidnapped by "bush whackers"—night raiders during the Civil War era near Diamond, Missouri. The raiders knew the slave Mary would bring a good price, but the baby was tiny and sickly looking, so they kept Mary and dropped the little baby by the roadside. Fortunately for baby George, his owner, Moses Carver, came looking for the baby and his mother. He recovered only baby George.

The Carvers were kind people and loved George and his five-year-old brother, Jim. On December 18, 1865, the 13th Amendment to the Constitution went into effect, so the Carvers decided to raise the boys as their own children. Though it was unusual for white parents to raise Black children, the neighbors respected Moses Carver because of his prosperity. Moses raised racehorses that he trained for future track racing.

George remembered the Carvers as loving parents; he also said, "There are so many things, that naturally, I erased from my mind. There are so many things that an orphan child does not want to remember."[31] George's big brother, Jim, helped Moses with the demanding work in the fields, while George, a frail and sickly little boy, helped Mrs. Carver in the kitchen with cooking meals, mending clothes, and tending the garden.

Early on, George showed a special interest in the plants he tended. He experimented with a variety of soils and growing conditions. Local people soon called him the "Plant Doctor" and sought his advice on growing their own plants and flowers. The Carvers encouraged George's rare gift and talents as the young boy explored the nearby fields and woods collecting various specimens of many plants and creatures.

After encountering some of George's live specimens, however, Mrs. Carver made sure he emptied his pockets before coming into the house. George said about the early days of his life, "I wanted to know every strange stone, flower, insect, bird, or beast."[31a] The only reference book available at the time was *Webster's Elementary Spelling Book,* a book that didn't begin to satisfy George's advanced questions.

George and his brother Jim went to church regularly, and by the time he was ten, George had become a Christian. Throughout his life he believed first and foremost that God created everything—he linked his views of nature to his belief in God as the Creator.

Before the Civil War, laws prohibited teaching slaves to read and write. After the war ended in 1865, however, Jim and George enrolled in a local school that met in the church where they worshipped. The school turned them away later because they were black. In 1876, the Carvers provided a tutor for George, backing up his desire to learn. But the tutor didn't have the knowledge to satisfy him. He tried other nearby schools, finally ending up in Fort Scott, Kansas. Then, after a violent episode involving a rape charge concerning a black man and subsequent hanging, George fled the town in fear.

At that time, George traveled to various places (and schools) in Kansas, supporting himself with the domestic skills he learned from Mrs. Carver. By 1885, George was ready for college, and once more, had trouble finding a college that would accept him.

In the meantime, George became a homesteader and claimed 160 acres of land under the Homestead Act of 1862. He built himself a sod house and added a conservatory filled with native plants. However, he became frustrated by the effects of the climate on the vegetables and other crops he planted. The winters were harsh on his crops—especially when water was scarce. Finally, he gave up being a homesteader and left Ness County in 1889.

From Ness County, George traveled north to Winterset, Iowa, and then to Ames, Iowa, where he entered the Iowa State College of Agriculture and Mechanical Arts. Prior to his enrollment, George had participated in the art department. He painted many fine pictures of horticultural subjects; ultimately, though, he knew it would be hard to support himself as an artist.

One professor said of George, "Carver is by all means the ablest student we have."[31b] The professor referred in part to George's ability to graft plants, to cross-fertilize plants (combining cells from two different plants), and to create hybrids (cross-fertilizing different plants to form new ones). George graduated in 1894 with a bachelor of agriculture degree.

In March, 1896, he received a letter from Booker T. Washington, Principal of the Tuskegee Institute in Alabama, inviting George to be on the faculty there. He wanted him to head up the school's new agriculture department. George accepted the offer from Washington and plunged into his work. Tuskegee's agricultural experimental station, which was just ten acres, thrived under Carver's direction. He was concerned, however, with the worn-out condition of much soil in the South from repeated plantings of cotton. He said, "The average farmer goes on trying to raise cotton in the same old way, which means nothing but failure, more or less, for him."[31c] The solution, for Carver, was threefold: 1) Crop rotation to enrich the soil, 2) The use of organic fertilizer to replace the soil's lost nutrients, and 3) The introduction of new crops that farmers could sell on the market as well as serve at their own kitchen tables.

As they implemented these ideas, the students planted crops such as peanuts, sweet potatoes, black-eyed peas, alfalfa, velvet beans, and soybeans. Carver also took his agricultural knowledge to the rural poor farmer in the South. Whatever means he could use to help the poor Southern farmer, Carver attempted. He set up his own laboratory early on in Tuskegee. One of the products he made was "peanut milk," better known now as "peanut butter." In fact, Carver came up with a whole list of uses for the peanut: Peanut milk, Peanut candy, Instant coffee, Cosmetics, and Breakfast food

The rest of Carver's days after age 60 were packed full of conducting experiments, teaching classes, and giving speeches all over the country. He was truly a great scientist and American who never stopped growing mentally and spiritually. As his good friend Henry Ford said in 1942,"In my opinion, Professor Carver has taken Thomas Edison's place as the world's greatest living scientist."[31d]

George Washington Carver accomplished many things with a life that started out with so little promise. Although Tuskegee Institute boasts a monument of Carver on its grounds, the greatest monument is the man himself: his life and a legacy that will remain forever.

My Own Spiritual Growth

After some years of married life and with two young children, my spirit was restless. I wondered if life offered more than I had experienced. As if in answer to an unspoken prayer, a minister my husband knew appeared at our door one evening shortly before Christmas. We invited him in, and almost immediately, he started asking me questions like, "Do you know that God loves you and sent His Son Jesus Christ to die for your sins?" he queried. Well, I didn't know that at the time but I believed what Reverend Olney told me.

Before long, he told me to kneel in prayer and ask the Lord to forgive my sins and come into my life, which I did. At once, I was filled with a wonderful peace and joy—I knew the Lord heard and answered my prayer. That night marked a turning point in my spiritual life. It was as though I passed from death to life. My life has taken an upward turn ever since as I sense the Lord's peace and presence in my daily life.

"The woods are lovely, dark and deep.
But I have promises to keep,
And miles to go before I sleep,
And miles to go before I sleep."

Robert Frost (1874-1963)
Stopping by Woods on a Snowy Evening

---

[31]*George Washington Carver: Botanist and Ecologist* .Lois P. Nicholson. Chelsea House Publishers, 1984, pp. 10, [31a]12, [31b]13, [31c]26, [31d]33, 176.

CHAPTER TWENTY-FIVE

I DO HAVE A CHOICE

"Doing What You Want"
"Life does not give itself to one who tries to keep all its advantages at once. I have often thought morality may perhaps consistsolely in the courage of making a choice."

Leon Blum, (1872-1950)
"On Marriage"

Nathaniel Hawthorne, Obsession With Guilt (1804-1864)

From an early age, Nathaniel Hawthorne wanted to be a writer, but he needed money to support his craft. He once wrote his mother, "I don't see that there's anything left for me but to be an author. How would you like some day to see a whole shelf of books, written by your son with 'Hawthorne's Works' printed on their backs?"[32]

Many of Nathaniel Hawthorne's stories revolve around the theme of guilt. Even at an early age, Hawthorne was aware of John Ha{w}thorne, an ancestor and one of the judges at the Salem Witch Trials. From the time of his birth in Salem, Massachusetts, in 1804, Hawthorne brooded about his Puritan past and the harshness with which the Puritans punished those, like the Quakers, of a different religious persuasion from theirs.

Hawthorne pictures the ancestor of his family, William Ha{w}thorne, who arrived in 1630, "The bearded sable-cloaked and steeple-crowned progenitor" in the preamble to *The Scarlet Letter.* In this book, Hawthorne takes pains to point out the minister's guilt, as well as Hester Prynne's, who wears the scarlet "A."

When Hawthorne was four years old, his father, Captain Nathaniel Hawthorne died of yellow fever in Surinam, Dutch New Guiana, leaving his widow and three young children dependent on their relatives. Until Nathaniel was twelve, he lived with his mother and two sisters in the house of his mother's family, the Mannings. He was a typical young boy before he injured his foot at the age of nine and could no longer play active sports.

During this time, Nathaniel stayed indoors and began to read numerous books, especially the works of Sir Walter Scott, John Bunyan, and Shakespeare. As his foot injury improved, the young boy once again participated in outdoor activities. He also enjoyed visiting his uncle's home in Raymond, Maine. Here, he relished outdoor life, playing in the abundant forests that fed his active imagination and proved useful in his later stories. By the time he needed to prepare for college, his family moved back to Salem so Nathaniel could be tutored. But the three years he spent in Raymond were the happiest years of his childhood, although he admitted he first formed "the cursed habit of solitude" there.

Two years later, in 1821, when Hawthorne was seventeen, he entered Bowdoin College, a small country college in Maine. Several of Hawthorne's fellow students later became famous men. The poet, Henry Wadsworth Longfellow, was a classmate of Hawthorne's, but the two were never close. He became good friends, however, with a future U.S. President, Franklin Pierce.

He did not lead a distinguished college life and even admitted that he was an "idle" student. After leaving college, Hawthorne returned to his mother's house in Salem where he retreated and endeavored to write. He did write one story titled *Fanshawe: A Tale* and published it at his own expense. When the book copies did not sell, the author picked up all the unsold copies and retired from public view. His sister, Louisa, brought her brother's meals to him in his room—in fact, each member of the family ate their meals in their rooms.

Hawthorne took a vacation each summer, traveling to some place along the coast. Salem's days as a port were over and odd personages, old men and women, moved about the town, giving rise to all manner of strange tales.

At last, Hawthorne got a break from a Boston Publisher, Samuel Goodrich. Goodrich had read *Fanshawe* and when the young author sent a story titled "Young Provincial," Goodrich printed it in the 1830 issue of his magazine *The Token.* Hawthorne continued to contribute anonymously to the magazine, and in 1836, he became editor, through Goodrich, of the *American Magazine of Useful and Entertaining Knowledge.*

For four months Hawthorne worked hard at his new job but was paid only twenty dollars. In March, 1837, at the age of thirty-three, he saw the first published series of his *Twice-Told Tales.* His friend, Horatio Bridge, paid for the publishing. Bridge had paid for the printing with $250. Although the book was not a failure, it received scarce attention.

In the summer of 1837, Hawthorne visited Bridge in Maine and wrote in his notebook about the many characters he observed, describing them in detail. He had kept a notebook for years picturing various people he observed for use in subsequent future writings.

He still had no definite income and a friend helped him locate a job at the Boston Custom House in 1839 as a measurer of salt, coal and other items. For a writer with an active imagination, the work was dull and after two years, Hawthorne left and joined the "Brook Farm Community," a project of Emerson and the Transcendentalists. After a few months, he left the community where he shoveled manure and milked cows.

Following these dismal times for Hawthorne, he met an attractive young lady from a fine Boston family by the name of Sophia Peabody. Sophia, an artist, made drawings to illustrate his stories, and the two were immediately attracted to each other. Two years later, in July 1841, the two married and enjoyed a happy married life. Their first home was in the "Old Manse" in Concord, Massachusetts, the home of Emerson, and Ripley, who owned the home. They lived frugally sometimes having just milk, bread, and fruit for dinner while Sophia danced to the tunes of a music box.

When Sophia had guests, Hawthorne stalked through the hall with an old hat pulled down over his eyes appearing like the recluse he pretended to be. During this time, he wrote allegorical essays and short stories for *The Democratic Review*, but he was dissatisfied with his work.

Hawthorne needed some kind of job, however, and accepted a job at the Salem Custom House in 1846. The unhappiness of not writing weighed on him heavily, but at least the family had money coming in. When a few years later he had to give up his dismal job by a new government administration (in 1849), he said, "God bless my enemies, say I. If it had not been for their kind services, I might have been in the Surveyor's Room this day!"[32a]

The family moved to Lenox, Massachusetts to a little red cottage on a lonely farm when they left the "Old Manse" in 1849. Sophia had saved some money and announced to her surprised husband, "Now you can write your romance."[32b]

At this time, Hawthorne had two children, a daughter, Una, and a son, Julian. In 1850, the red cottage and the isolation of the farm provided a perfect setting for him to complete *The Scarlet Letter,* started some years before. Earlier, in 1837, Hawthorne had written a story about the Puritans; he had mentioned the letter "A" worn as a symbol of a woman accused of that crime. Those previous pages were expanded into a full-length book, and within ten days following publication, two thousand copies were sold.

By now, Hawthorne's reputation as a fiction writer had risen steadily. He wrote numerous other stories like *The House of Seven Gables, The Blithedale Romance,* and *Twice-Told Tales,* a collection of short stories, but none of them approached *The Scarlet Letter* in popularity as well as artistic value.

Two themes that predominate not only in *Twice-Told Tales,* but also in most of Hawthorne's writing are: (1) In every human heart lurks "a germ of evil," and (2) through indulgence of any isolating trait a person may fail to establish or may lapse from "life-giving sympathy" with human kind.

Hawthorne died in his sleep on May 10, 1864, while on a walking trip with his friend, Franklin Pierce. As much as he could in his life, he chose to spend his time writing; when the family needed money to live, however, he reluctantly worked at places like the Custom House in Salem.

If his wife had not made it possible with the purchase of the Red Cottage, we might not have *The Scarlet Letter,* the novel many critics during Hawthorne's lifetime consider the greatest American novel ever written.

Hawthorne's reputation has not declined today. He appeals, in particular, to contemporary literary people in two regards: 1) He explored psychological and moral aberrations of the private world of the individual, and 2) He used symbolic techniques in storytelling. No doubt Hawthorne would be amazed at this assessment of his work, although from an early age, that was his desire.

Making Choices

Each day we have choices to make—some yield small results and have little effect on our lives; others can be life changing .

Some years ago, I faced a big decision. The blond, blue-eyed man I was dating had proposed marriage, but I had other plans for my life. We had flown to Connecticut so I could meet his parents. They were wonderful people, and his mother and I got along "famously."

I agonized over my decision. I wanted to finish college so I could find a good job and a career. However, when my friend said, "I don't want to wait that long," I made up my mind quickly. Not wanting to lose him, I said, "Yes" to his offer. We were married a short time later.

This decision turned out to be one of the best I ever made; and I still finished college some years later, reaping both benefits of my decision—marriage and college graduation.

"Two roads converged in a yellow wood,
And sorry I could not travel both
And be one traveler, long I stood
And looked down one as far as I could
To where it bent in the undergrowth;

Then took the other, as just as fair,
And having perhaps the better claim,
Because it was grassy and wanted wear;
Though as for that the passing there
Had worn them really about the same,

And both that morning equally lay
In leaves no step had trodden black,
Oh, I kept the first for another day!
Yet knowing how way leads on to way,
I doubted if I should ever come back.

I shall be telling this with a sigh
Somewhere ages and ages hence;
Two roads diverged in a wood, and I—
I took the one less traveled by,
And that has made all the difference."
"The Road Not Taken"
Robert Frost (1874-1963)

[32]*Famous New England Authors. Laura Benet.* Dodd, Mead and Company. New York, 1970, pp. 20, [32a]22, [32b]23.

CHAPTER TWENTY-SIX

ATTAINING A SENSE OF ACCOMPLISHMENT AND SELF CONFIDENCE

"I can do this!"

"The desire accomplished is sweet to the soul."
Proverbs 13:19, O.T., NIV

Robert Fulton, Inventor of the Steamboat (1765-1815)

"My head is so full of original notions that there is no vacant chamber to store away the contents of dusty books," nine-year-old Robert Fulton confessed to his mother after another reprimand from his teacher.[33]

Robert was born in the colony of Pennsylvania, part of British North America, on November 14, 1765. The next to last of five children, Robert had three older sisters, Betsy, Polly, and Belle, plus a younger brother, Abraham.

One person who understood Robert, however, was William Henry, a family friend and inventor. He recognized Robert's bright mind and encouraged him wherever possible. Robert's father was a tailor in Lancaster, Pennsylvania; then he tried farming but the soil was poor, so he came back to Lancaster and to his weaving loom. Sadly, though, in 1774, Mr. Fulton died and six-year-old Robert became the head of the household.

Robert always found plenty to do in Lancaster, which bordered on the Conestoga Road, where travelers loaded up with supplies before heading west to the territory beyond the thirteen colonies. One of the things Robert enjoyed was visiting the chemist's shop. The chemist always kept a supply of mercury, or quicksilver, as some people called it. Robert liked to experiment with this strange element. One of the things Robert might have done with the quicksilver was to pour some in a glass tube and watch the thin strand climb in the tube as the day got warmer. Robert's friends called him "Quicksilver Bob" because of the way his mind moved and changed in a flash.

In 1775, when Robert was ten, the American Revolution began and Lancaster overflowed with soldiers and Revolutionary leaders like Thomas Paine and John Hancock. While the times excited ten-year-old Robert, they also saddened him with reports of battles at Bunker Hill, Brandywine, and Freeman's Farm.

Robert moved to Philadelphia to find work at the age of sixteen. He soon began to apprentice as a silversmith. He liked the work of molding and shaping silver but he didn't like working for someone else; so before long, he set up his own shop where he applied his artistic talents painting miniature portraits for the fashionable gold and silver lockets of the day. When he turned twenty-one, he had saved enough money to buy some farm land for his mother and planned on traveling to London to study with Benjamin West, a famous American artist living in London.

Robert's ship crossing required weeks, even months, through tumultuous seas, violent storms, and thick fogs. Sometimes the sails tore and the food rotted. Drinking water was rationed. Even so, at times there was little enough water to drink, and bed bugs were commonplace.

In London, Robert tried various ways to earn a living using his artistic and inventive skills, but he still managed to just scrape by. In the meantime, Robert worked out some exciting plans to build a canal. But when he showed his plans to Englishmen, they exhibited little interest. Their lack of interest led him to leave for France, hoping for a better reception.

Soon, however, Robert had another idea: to construct a "boat fish," or submarine. He created a design for a submarine and called it "Nautilus." He worked out all the details and problems for the vessel, including how to make it sink. He even designed a periscope that stuck up above the ship and could look in all directions. Robert liked Paris where the people were much livelier than the people in London. All went well with his "bateau-poisson," or boat fish, as the French called it.[33a]

When Robert met Robert Livingston in Paris, however, everything began to change for him. Livingston asked Robert to work with him on a Hudson River project promoting the use of a steamboat. In his designs, Robert soon realized the best idea involved a paddle wheel to propel the boat through the water. The final version was going to be six-feet wide and 90 feet long. The boat would travel at eight miles an hour upstream, covering the 140 miles. Robert continued to make changes on the boat.

Back in the United States, Robert kept modifying and changing the steamboat plans. He would then send a quick note up-river to Livingston's estate, *Clermont,* telling him things like "decided to modify the design of the hull, keeping a narrow width of 13 feet and extending the length to 150 feet."[33b] The sides of the boat were to be five feet high at the deck.

Robert also told Livingston the boat could accommodate fifty paying customers. He estimated the boat could make four trips a week between New York and Albany, so they could expect to earn $32,000 a year after subtracting the cost of coal. The steamboat's hull received its first coat of gray paint by the end of May, 1807. Then, in July, the boat was moved to another shipyard along the East River where the boat's engine was to be installed by the second week in the month.

At last, the day of departure arrived on August 17 when Fulton's "Steamboat" was to begin its maiden voyage up the Hudson River toward Albany. Then the crowd along the river began to jeer and make fun of the odd-looking boat with its side paddle wheels calling it, "Fulton's Folly." Livingston had also invited several guests for the maiden voyage.[33c]

Most of the guests persuaded to go on the first trip of the *Clermont* steamboat feared for their lives. Nevertheless, Robert watched as the people boarded the boat, and he said later, "My friends were in groups on the deck. There was anxiety mixed with fear among them. They were silent, sad, and weary. I read in their looks nothing but disaster."[33d] As the ship pulled away from the dock, the passengers relaxed, and the following day, it reached Livingston's Clermont Estate. It traveled five miles an hour.

Both Robert Fulton and Robert Livingston became wealthy men due to the proceeds from the steamboat. Although in his forties, Robert Fulton now felt comfortable enough to marry, which he did on January 7, 1808, when he married Livingston's young cousin Harriet. Fulton was satisfied with his steamboat but continued to change it and use it on many other American waterways, including the Mississippi River.

Fulton died following a tragic accident on the ice in 1815. He was only forty-nine years old but had lived long enough to enjoy a sense of accomplishment with his launching of the *Clermont* some years earlier.

An Accomplishment of My Own

After a few years of editing book manuscripts for a large publisher, I was ready to write a book of my own. At the time, I belonged to a small writer's critique group with three or four other people.

We met in my spacious apartment sitting on brown and beige upholstered rattan chairs around a circular, glass-topped rattan table. Two of the women were working on novels, the rest of us on non-fiction articles and books. The publisher I worked for had given me an opportunity to submit two chapters of a biography, but this was my first effort at writing one, so I was most anxious about doing it right.

As usual that night, the others tore my work apart: Gloria said, "It needs to be more conversational," and Rita suggested, "Put more action into it." Justified in what they said, their words cut into me like daggers and overwhelmed me with discouragement. After they left, I half-heartedly said a prayer asking God to help me. Then, I sat down at the computer and re-wrote my chapters, and the following day, sent them off to the publisher.

A couple of weeks went by, and I decided to call one of the publisher's assistants to find out the manuscript status. James told me, "I think Barbara wants more dialogue, etc. But she likes what you have." My heart began to soar. They were going to accept my manuscript with some changes!

Soon, I made the suggested changes and within a few months the book was published. You can still find my first biography, *The Life of D.L. Moody* at many bookstores. What a sense of accomplishment I felt to have my first book published—nothing that happened after that could compare with it.

"Whatever you can do or dream you can, begin it."
Johann Wolfgang von Goethe (1749-1832)

[33]*A Head Full of Notions: A Story about Robert Fulton.* Andy Russell Bowen. Carol Rhoda Books, Inc., Minneapolis, 1997, pp. 7, [33a]29, [33b]45, [33c]48, [33d]48,

CHAPTER TWENTY-SEVEN

TAKING A CLASS

"I'm not too old to learn"

"Give me a young man in whom there is something of the old, and an old man with something of the young; guided so, a man may grow old in body, but never in mind."

Marcus Terantino Varro, (116-27 B.C.)
De Senectute, XI

Davy Crockett, Trail Blazer (1786-1836)

Davy Crockett's feats have given rise to many legends: How he killed a bear when he was three years old; how he "grinned" down savage animals armed only with his strong grip and abundant charm; and how he never failed to hit a bull's eye with "Ol' Betsey," his long rifle.[34] Some of these legends were true, some were not. But he was a trail-blazing pioneer of the vanishing frontier and an excellent marksman.

Davy Crockett was born on a farm on Big Limestone Creek in Greene County, Tennessee on August 17, 1786. His ancestors came from Irish stock, settling in North Carolina before the American Revolution. Davy's grandfather, David Crockett, moved onto the frontier in Eastern Tennessee in the 1770's where warring Indians killed him. Davy also had eight brothers and sisters.

His father operated a tavern (after failing as a hog farmer and miller) on the wagon road between Knoxville, Tennessee, and Abingdon, Virginia. The tavern also doubled as an Inn where wagon drivers could spend the night sleeping three and four to a bed. Davy relished listening to all the "Tall Tales" of the travelers who stayed at the tavern. In fact, he began developing his own "Tall Tales."

As he grew, Davy also developed his skills as a woodsman and hunter. He became renowned for being a crack shot. He was able to shoot the wick off a candle at 300 feet; once, he killed 47 bears in a single month.

At thirteen, Davy's father wanted him to go to school. Before long, however, he made a powerful enemy in the school bully. In order to escape his father's punishment for scratching the boy's face, as Davy said, "I scratched his face all to a flitter jig," he ran away to Virginia.[34a] He soon found work as a farmhand and received a small compensation.

When he reached the age of 18, however, Davy wanted to get married. Unfortunately, he had a couple of unhappy romances—that is, the girl ended up with someone else. After the second romantic breakup, Davy wrote, "My heart was bruised, and my spirits were broken down."[34b]

Things worked out for Davy, though, when he met Polly (Mary) Finley in 1806 at a community dance party. This time, everything happened in his favor. Polly had broken up with another young man so she could marry Davy. Just before he met her, however, he decided to return to school so he could at least learn to read and write. He was already eighteen, but he realized his need for some schooling. He stayed at his studies for six months, then left school for good. In just a few months after they met, Polly and Davy were married. They soon had two sons, John Wesley and William Crockett, and a daughter, Margaret. Davy's crack marksmanship kept the family well supplied with deer, rabbits, and other small game.

In 1813, Creek Warriors, or "Red Sticks" as the settlers called the Creek Indians, went on the warpath south of the Crockett's Elk River County. However, when a Red Stick war party crashed Fort Mims in Alabama and massacred more than five hundred settlers, the whites organized a militia with General Andrew Jackson in command. Davy signed up to be a militia scout. Though he didn't distinguish himself in that role, his storytelling amused everyone, including General Jackson.

Davy continued his days as an explorer and frontiersman; he wasn't cut out to be a farmer. Before long, though, he did venture into politics. He became a magistrate and justice of the peace. Soon, the local militia elected him as their colonel. Then some of his friends persuaded Davy to run for the Tennessee State Legislature. All he knew to do for speeches was to tell his humorous, folksy stories when asked to give a speech. Following his speech, he offered the hard-working farmers free drinks at the liquor stand. Davy's opponent followed him to the "stump," but usually the crowd had dispersed by then—and Davy ended up winning the election by a landslide. He ran and lost a subsequent election bid and returned to his real loves: hunting and following new wilderness ventures.

Davy was in and out of politics for a few years, even serving in national politics, but afterward, he always returned to his roots of hunting and exploring the wilderness. His next venture lay in the Texas wilderness. Texas lay outside U.S. boundaries, and Davy hoped for a new beginning for his life. However, Texas was controlled by Mexico. Many of the American-born residents clamored for independence from Mexico.

The situation between the Americans and the Mexicans finally culminated at the Alamo, formerly an old Spanish mission. Davy Crockett was among the Americans in the Alamo as they fought for an independent Texas. So, on February 23, 1836, Santa Ana, the Mexican leader vowed the Americans "would be given no quarter" but would "be killed to the last man"—the Texans remained firm.[34c] The Alamo defenders ultimately lost the battle due to low ammunition and fewer fighting men. On March 6, as the last defender was slain, the Mexicans gained control of the Alamo.

Davy Crockett was one of the last defenders to die, according to legend. His gun, Ol' Betsey, was found "bloodied and broken from the final moments of hand-to-hand fighting."[34d] To the end, however, Davy Crockett retained a fighting spirit. His love of adventure and the wilderness made him a perfect man for the time he lived in. His favorite saying, reflecting his back woods' simplicity and honesty was, "Be always sure you're right, then go ahead."[34e]

Taking a Class

When I needed five more hours of credit, I decided to take a creative writing class with this rather eccentric professor, Dr. Beavers. He lived on a small farm and brought eggs to class from his laying hens—of course, he charged for the eggs. The unusual feature about his class was that the student could determine his or her grade—they just had to show they deserved it.

About three or four weeks before the end of the class, I still hadn't decided on a project. Then, I had a bright idea: I would enter a writing contest I saw advertised. So, I put an article together for *Liberty* Magazine about how America's government was based on Calvinistic principles and sent it off to the magazine.

"Good," I thought, "at least I have earned my 'A.'" A couple of weeks went by, and almost the last day of class, I checked my home mailbox. Much to my surprise, I had a letter and a check for $100 from *Liberty* magazine. The letter said I hadn't won anything in the contest, but they bought my article. What a joy and encouragement that was to me. Dr. Beavers was pleased as well and said he was justified in giving me the grade of "A" in creative writing.

"If wrinkles must be written upon our brows, let them not be written upon our hearts.The spirit should not grow old."

James A. Garfield, 20th U.S. President

(1831-1881)

[34]*Davy Crockett.* Daniel E. Harmon. Chelsea House Publishers, Stockton, NJ, 2002, pp. 18, [34a]11, [34b]17, [34c]56, [34d]57, [34e]59.

Chapter Twenty-eight

Changing Habits for the Better

"This is only making things worse"

"Chaos often breeds life, when order breeds habit."
The Education of Henry Adams
Henry Brooke Adams (1838-1918)

Cyrus McCormick, Inventor of the Reaper (1809-1884)

Sweat poured off the body of fifteen-year-old Cyrus McCormick as he rhythmically cut the wheat in his father's fields with a curve-handled scythe. The sun was hot and Cyrus wanted to rest, but he still had another one to two acres to cut before the day was over. He thought to himself, "There must be a way to use horses to cut and harvest wheat."[35]

As he experimented with various tools in his father's log blacksmith shop later on in the evening, the thought came back of designing a reaper that used horses instead of human labor. His father had already designed a number of farm inventions but a workable reaper eluded him.

Cyrus Hall McCormick was born on his father's farm on February 15, 1809. Cyrus was the first child of Robert and Mary Ann or "Polly" McCormick. Walnut Grove, the McCormick Farm, was located in Rockbridge County, Virginia. Later on, as he prospered, Robert owned 1200 acres of fertile farmland. The nearest town, Staunton, was eighteen miles north of the farm. The Atlantic Ocean lay 100 miles due east.

In addition to farming, Robert also owned two gristmills, two saw mills, a smelting furnace, a distillery, and a blacksmith shop. Robert was a talented inventor as well with an unusual aptitude in mechanics. He invented new types of farm machinery: a hemp brake, a clover huller, a bellows, and a threshing machine. Only twenty-four feet square with an uneven floor, the blacksmith shop had a forge on each side of the chimney enabling two men to work hot metal at the same time.

Cyrus wrote later, "My father was both mechanical and inventive, and could and did at that time use the tools of his shop in making any piece of machinery he wanted. He invented, made, and patented several more or less valuable agricultural implements...but most of his inventions dropped into disuse after the lapse of some years."[35a]

When Cyrus was five years old, he came down with yellow fever. Both his mother's parents and brother had already died from the deadly disease. The doctor left a "lancet" at the McCormick home, telling Robert to "bleed" his young son. Robert, however, refused; instead, he immersed the boy in hot baths containing bitter herbs and whiskey and giving him hot tea to drink. He completely recovered a short time later.

Prior to adolescence, at around the age of eight, Cyrus attended Old Field School not far from the McCormick farm; his mother and father also taught him at home. He received daily instruction in Scripture, catechism, and other spiritual studies from his Scotch-Irish Presbyterian parents. His father also taught him to use the tools in his blacksmith shop as well as involving him in business operations. Some of Cyrus' schoolbooks were: *Murray's Grammar, Dilworth's Arithmetic, Webster's Spelling Book, Adam's Geography,* and the *New York Primer.*

As he grew to adolescence, Cyrus was six feet, two inches tall, with a muscular build but having small hands and feet. At this time, the young man gave more attention to devising a reaping machine that worked. To do so, he needed to overcome the problems his father encountered: the machine needed to cut the ripe grain, but also handle and deliver the cut grain.

Cyrus' first success with a reaper prototype came in July 1831. The machine was pulled by a single horse, guided by a rider. The horse walked through previously cut stubble before the right side of a crosswise-extending cutter bar with an associated reciprocating blade, which the horse drew; it cut a swath through ripe grain on the left side.

As the cutter bar advanced and the grain cut, the grain moved back and fell upon a horizontal platform trailing behind the cutter bar. The cut grain was raked by hand off the platform to the open (right) or stubble side (behind the horse) by a raker who walked alongside the machine.

Cyrus' bigger job now was to convince farmers for the need of his new machine. He continued to make improvements on it even at a time when other people were also inventing reapers and getting patents on them. However, McCormick's design was superior to the others.

Riding his horse home one day, the thought came to Cyrus, "Perhaps I may make a million dollars from this reaper."[35b] He said in later years, "This thought was so enormous that it seemed like a dream—like dwelling in the clouds—so remote, so unattainable, so exalted, so visionary."[35c]

Cyrus decided at that point to create a business from his reaper. He couldn't be content building a few reapers in his father's blacksmith's shop. He started to advertise his reaper; although this was unheard of in the 1830's. In the meantime, Cyrus paid thirty dollars to the U.S. Treasury and on June 21, 1834, obtained a patent on his reaper.

McCormick was not alone in his invention. In fact, roughly one hundred other individuals had also invented some type of reaper. A serious competitor, Obed Hussey, posed a dire threat to McCormick's number one position. As it turned out, after several side-by-side trials of the two reapers, Cyrus' reaper always operated more efficiently. After while, Hussey was past history.

McCormick's problem now was to locate a more convenient manufacturing location. Virginia and anywhere on the East Coast was too far away from the "Great Plains" area of the country. The inventor finally settled on Chicago as the best location to produced his machine.

In addition to finding a suitable location, McCormick still had to overcome the farmers' skepticism. To overcome this last obstacle, McCormick devised a credit plan whereby a farmer could put so much toward the Reaper's purchase, then pay the rest after harvest. After solving a number of problems with his new plan, it proved to be a turning point for producing and selling the Reaper.

In 1846, Cyrus began to enjoy success with his Reaper. As H.E. Towner of Will County, Illinois, said in July 1846, "I consider it {the McCormick Reaper} to the western country the most important invention of the age, and that it will greatly increase the product of the country, not being able without it to reap so much as can be sown."[36]

More praise and endorsement came from the editor of the *Chicago Daily Journal,* who said the McCormick Reaper "Will cut from 15 to 20 acres per day, which is as decided an advantage as the Magnetic Telegraph is on steam. These machines are highly useful in this state, where the harvest is large, while the means of saving it is disproportionately small."[36a]

Later on, McCormick also sold reapers in Europe with some success. England and France even decorated him for his invention. From the beginning of his business of manufacturing the reaper, he had various problems: with defective reapers, inadequate business partners, etc., but his tough Scotch-Irish ancestry served him well. He was a stern, self-disciplined man who always refused to take the easy way out. As he persevered in business and solved his problems, his business prospered, and he became very wealthy. Toward the end of his life, he contributed to a Presbyterian Seminary in Chicago (now called McCormick Seminary), and endowed a chair in Washington and Lee University in Virginia.

All the way along his amazing journey to power and wealth, McCormick was forced to change the way he thought about doing things—his "fixed" habits.

He had to continually solve the problems caused by manufacturing and distribution. In his lifetime, he manufactured more than six million reapers, continually making improvements on his original reaper. The dream he had earlier about becoming wealthy and successful had come true.

PROCRASTINATION

Do you struggle with procrastination? Like Scarlet O'Hara, do you tell yourself, "I'll think about that tomorrow?" Do you put off unpleasant tasks like cleaning the basement or doing your income tax because you just don't feel like doing them?

I must confess to being a procrastinator—but it's not good to be one! Procrastination means "to put off doing something, especially out of habitual carelessness or laziness." It also means "to postpone or delay needlessly doing a task until tomorrow." Most people procrastinate at some time in their lives.

Similar to many people, I procrastinate because a task is either unpleasant or overwhelming. But I have discovered some ways to combat this bad habit. In addition, there is also a "pay off" and a sense of relief when I complete a task. If the task seems overwhelming, I break it into three or four stages, doing a little at a time. I can even clean the refrigerator one shelf at a time!

However, for the unpleasant tasks like cleaning bathrooms, I try to play some enjoyable music or watch something else on a small, portable appliance. I even use a kitchen timer to time myself to accomplish something.

Most important of all, when I finish a dreaded task, I reward myself—maybe by stopping at a new salad bar, buying something new, or perhaps taking a long walk on a cool evening.

I'm happy to report that, although not completely cured, I have made progress in overcoming this troublesome habit. So, I can honestly say that while procrastination has been called "the thief of time," today it's not stealing much of mine!

Habits
"Sow a thought, and you reap an act;
Sow an act, and you reap a habit;
Sow a habit, and you reap a character;
Sow a character, and you reap a destiny."
Quoted by Samuel Smiles (1812-1904)
In *Life and Labor* (1887)

Cyrus McCormick and the Mechanical Reaper. Lisa J. Aldrich. Morgan Reynolds Publishing, Inc., Greensboro, N.C., 2002, pp. 9, 11,12, 16.

[35]*Icons of Invention,* Col. I, John W. Klooster, 2009, pp. 9, [35a]11,12; [35b]28; [35c]28; [35d]51; [36]51; [36a]52

Chapter Twenty-nine

Accepting What Cannot Be Changed

"Time to Get Over This"

"God, give us grace to accept with serenity the things that cannot be changed, courage to change the things which should be changed, and the wisdom to know the difference."

Reinhold Niebuhr (1892-1971)

Louisa May Alcott, Author, *Little Women* (1832-1888)

On a cold December afternoon in 1862, Louisa May Alcott boarded a train in Concord, Massachusetts, headed for Boston and Washington, D.C. After three hard days of travel, she would report for duty as a Civil War nurse.

Louisa was born on November 29, 1832, in Germantown, Pennsylvania, the oldest daughter of (Amos) Bronson Alcott, a dreamer, educational reformer and fervent intellectual, and {Abba} May, wise and kind, resourceful and energetic, born of old New England stock. Together, they would raise four daughters on a "shoe string" existence.

Louisa returned from her war experience still recovering from a bout with typhoid fever. The doctors had treated her with calomel, a purgative drug containing mercury. Her father came to the hospital to take her to their home in   Concord. The Alcott's home in Concord was called "Hillside," and Louisa had her own room where she began to write a piece called "Hospital Sketches." It was published in 1963 in *The Commonwealth*, a journal by reformers who advocated abolition. The piece was praised by many readers who said, "Graphically drawn" scenes as "fluent and sparkling with touches of quiet humor."[37]

Always concerned about her family, Louisa worried about her father's inability to hold a job. His unorthodox ideas on education would at first be received at a school, then his unconventional thoughts and methods would be looked down on. Finally, he and his family experienced ostracism, and they were often on the verge of poverty. In spite of his failings, Louisa adored her father.

After an unsuccessful time of the Alcotts living in a farming community called "Fruitlands," largely supported by Ralph Waldo Emerson and Henry Thoreau, and founded on transcendentalist thought, the community failed to produce sufficient crops to feed everyone, so it was closed.

Once more, the Alcotts lived on the edge of poverty. Their good friend, Emerson, however, paid for their rent for a year back in Concord. Louisa loved living in Concord with Thoreau as her teacher some of the time; he would lead his pupils on excursions through the woods pointing out aspects of wild life.

Thirteen-year-old Louisa thrived on these years in Concord. She even wrote plays, and with her sisters, produced them for neighbors and friends in the property's barn. She was a good seamstress, as well, and earned money sewing doll clothes for desiring patrons.

She also wrote melodramatic stories at the age of sixteen, which she sold for five and ten dollars apiece.

Sadly the Alcotts' time at Hillside came to an end, and Abba (Mrs. Alcott) was offered work in Boston as an official visitor to the poor. A brother of Mrs. Alcott's offered the family a place to live, so they moved to Boston. In the city, while Abba worked at her job, the younger girls attended school, Anna taught, and Louisa sewed, and even became a nursery governess for a time.

The family moved back to Concord later that year and bought a place with a small inheritance Abba Alcott received. Although Louisa had written small pieces during these years, she now began to write regularly in a special wing of their Concord home. During this time, too, sixteen-year-old Louisa struggled with her own thoughts of independence and the changeable emotions of her teenage years. She sensed herself destined for some kind of greatness, planned on accomplishing great things. She said, "by and by...don't care what"...teaching, sewing, acting, writing, anything to help the family, and I'll be rich and famous and happy before I die, see if I don't."[37a]

Louisa's predicament was difficult during these years. She didn't want to be compliant as a woman, marry, and raise a family, although that was expected of her. Actually, until the early twentieth century, women were regarded as the property of their husbands and could not own property, sign contracts, obtain credit, go into business, or control their earnings.

In 1860, Louisa's sister, Anna, married John Bridge Pratt; and Louisa's creative years began. For fifteen years she had had little success as a writer. Now, back in Concord and with her sister married, Louisa's writing started in earnest. She began a book called *Moods*, and another, called *Success*.

Then, one of her publishers, Thomas Niles of Roberts Brothers Publishing, urged her: "I think, Miss Alcott, that you could write a book for girls. I should like to see you try."[38] Even though Louisa objected, saying she knew more about boys than girls, she began writing *Little Women* in May 1868. Alcott's book was autobiographical, based on her own close-knit family.

The book was a great success and with the money she earned, Louisa provided comforts for her family that they could not have afforded otherwise. Then, Mr. Niles asked for a sequel, so Louisa started a book called *Old-fashioned Girls*. With the money she earned from *Little Women*, Louisa paid off all the family's old debts and made the family independent and comfortable.

Another book Louisa began was the sequel, or a second volume to *Little Women*. She started it in November 1868, and finished it by New Year's. The book turned out to be a runaway best seller as thirteen thousand copies sold almost immediately with *Little Women* appearing in every bookseller's window. Louisa May Alcott, almost overnight, was the most famous author in America. Royalties flooded in, assuring her and her family comfort beyond their wildest dreams. She was committed to caring for her family in the absence of her father's working ability.

Even as she toured Europe a short time later with May, her younger sister, Alcott discovered her fame had preceded her in England, France and other countries abroad where young readers reveled in her books. At the same time as her overwhelming success, her health began to fail.

She became bedridden in Brittany, France, because of tormenting pains in her legs and a continuing headache. The visiting British doctor recognized the symptoms as a result of mercury poisoning. The doctor prescribed wine to promote circulation, long woolen underwear to keep warm, and doses of iodine or potash as an antidote.

As Louisa and May traveled on to winter in Rome, they learned of the death of Anna's husband, John Pratt from mercury poisoning. Now, Louisa took it upon herself to care for Anna and her boys. She began another book called *Little Men*. Always, Louisa turned her sorrow and tragedies into writing.

Arriving back home, Louisa was greeted by her father and her publisher, Thomas Niles. They congratulated her on the success of *Little Men*—it was almost as wildly acclaimed as *Little Women*. She received countless invitations to speak from schools, colleges, and other groups; she could accept but few because of her failing health.

Louisa's mother died in 1877. Following her death, Louisa's father, Anna, Louisa, and Anna's sons went to live in Thoreau's house in Concord. May remained in Europe at the time of her mother's death and married Ernest Nieriker, a young Swiss. May died a year and a half later leaving to her sister, Louisa, her little girl Lulu, who was her namesake.

Now, Louisa was in charge of the Pratt boys and Lulu. The last book she wrote was *Jo's Boys*. The sorrow in her life overwhelmed her with two sisters, her brother-in-law, and mother all deceased. In the midst of her sorrow, however, she derived special comfort from little Lulu—who was a handful, but much like Louisa.

Louisa died on March 6, 1888, in her mid-fifties two days after her father. She was buried in Sleepy Hollow Cemetery near the graves of Emerson, Thoreau, and Hawthorne. When she realized early in life that she would have to be the "bread winner" in the family in her father's absence, instead of complaining about it, she accepted her "lot" in life and began to write to earn a living. She succeeded beyond her wildest dreams; however, if she had not had the incentive to spur her on, her greatest work *Little Women* might never have been written.

Steven's Death

In the course of writing this book, I faced a great sadness when my adult son, Steven, passed away from liver cancer.

For years, he had struggled with liver problems resulting from a bout with hepatitis. Early in 2011, he called one day from his home in New Mexico and said cheerfully, "Mom, I'm going to get a liver transplant. I qualify for it, and my insurance will cover it." I was so happy for him and rejoiced with him.

When he entered the hospital in California for the transplant, however, the doctors discovered a large tumor near the portal vein of his liver. Regrettably, he no longer qualified for a liver transplant and the doctors sent him home to die. He passed away in November of 2011.

Even though I have been greatly saddened by his death, I trust my heavenly Father to do what seems best in my life. Because of trusting Him, I have peace about Steven's death. I will see him again, and in the meantime, loving memories of the kind, gentle person he was comfort my heart. I have accepted what I cannot change. As a Scottish missionary, Amy Carmichael (1867-1951), said, "In the way of acceptance lies peace." She spoke a wonderful truth worth practicing in our lives.

[37]*Louisa May Alcott.* Kathleen Burke. Chelsea House Publishers, New York, 1988, pp. 22, [37a]45.
[38]*Famous New England Authors.* Laura Benet. Dodd, Mead, and Company, 1970, p. 88.

Afterword

As I look back over these chapters that deal with so many different topics, I am gratified that I've reached the end of my project.

My greatest desire is that you will be encouraged and helped in your own life's journey by these various people and topics. Life is a journey and it all "ties" together—the early stages, the middle stages, and the latter stages. If you stop growing and learning at any of these stages, your life will not be complete and you'll miss some important steps in your life.

Who knows what you can yet accomplish in your life if you but put your mind to it. As George Bernard Shaw in his play *Back to Methuselah* said, "You see things; and you say, 'Why?'But I dream things that never were; and I say, 'Why not?'"

About the Author

Bonnie C. Harvey is an author, editor, teacher, and speaker who holds a doctorate in English. She has written numerous biographies, conducts writing workshops, and is a former movie review editor and film critic.

Among her historical biographies are *Jane Addams: Nobel Prize Winner and Founder of Hull House, Daniel Webster: Liberty and Union, Now and Forever.*

In the past, she and her deceased husband have enjoyed a series of Siamese cats with improbable names like "Beau Joie," but cats are no longer part of her lifestyle. Instead, Bonnie acknowledges her "farming roots" by tending to house plants like Peace Lilies, African Violets, and an occasional hardy Orchid. She savors reading Mary Higgins Clark mysteries and likes to travel whenever possible. Her travels have taken her to England, Canada, Pifo, Ecuador, and Chosica, Peru. Bonnie lives in the Atlanta, Georgia area.

To contact Bonnie Harvey
for speaking engagements
email her at
BoncaH@aol.com

— To Order —

Living Life Twice: A Second Chance at Adulthood
by Bonnie C. Harvey

If unavailable at your favorite bookstore,
LangMarc Publishing will fill
your order within 24 hours.

—Postal Orders—
LangMarc Publishing
P.O. Box 90488
Austin, Texas 78709-0488
or call 1-800-864-1648
Order from LangMarc's secured website
www.langmarc.com

Living Life Twice
USA: $15.95 + $3 postage
Canada: $18.95 + $5 postage

Send _____ copies of *Living Life Twice* $15.95

Shipping $ 3.00

TX res. 8.25%   _____

Amount of Sale: _____

Send to: _____

_____

_____

Phone: _____

Check enclosed: _____

Credit Card # _____

Expiration: _____ Code: _____